Praise for *Our Lady o*

D0149940

"*This beautifully written book touches your soul. Anyone searching for peace will find the path to faith and forgiveness in* **Our Lady of Kibeho.**"

— **Amy Polasky,** the founder of LLI Academy of Foreign Affairs

"*If you believe that the genocide that happened in predominantly Catholic Rwanda was one of those isolated things that could never happen anywhere else—think again. This incredible book will open your eyes to how, from pure love, heaven warns us of the consequences of forgetting about God and pleads with us continually to begin anew a life closer to the Lord through prayer, penance, conversion, and preparation for the return of Christ.*"

— **Oscar I. Delgado,** film producer and the former Latin American Bureau Chief of NBC News

"*A fascinating account of the most recent apparition of Our Lady to receive Vatican recognition. The story of Kibeho is filled with the mystery of the conflict of good and evil, of the justice and mercy of God, of unanswerable questions of life leading us to take our refuge in the heart of the Holy Mother and in the hands of Divine Mercy. Like [Immaculée's] other [work],* **Left to Tell,** *you will never forget this book.*"

— **Fr. Benedict J. Groeschel,** Community of Franciscan Friars of the Renewal, Larchmont, New York

"*The appearances of the Virgin Mary in the little African village of Kibeho, Rwanda, is one of the most important apparitions in recent history and will take its place among other historical giants, like those of Guadalupe and Fátima. This book, however, is more than the story of an apparition. It's a remarkable story of how Rwanda, a country divided by ethnic hatreds and shattered by one of the bloodiest genocides in human history, is being reunited and healed through a singular faith in the enduring love of the Virgin Mary.*"

— **Drew Mariani,** the nationally syndicated talk-show host and award-winning writer, producer, and director

"Why did God send the Queen of Heaven and Earth, mother of Christ, and mother of all peoples to Kibeho, Rwanda? Why did the Blessed Virgin choose to come into the heart of rural Africa with messages for the entire world? Immaculée, like a flower that has sprung from the soil of Kibeho, has dedicated her life to addressing these questions and helping us to understand the messages the Blessed Mother delivered to three visionaries here, messages that echo the powerful truths of the gospel. The redeeming love of the Blessed Mother lives on in Kibeho and is here for the world to discover. Immaculée has captured that love in **Our Lady of Kibeho**. If you read this book, it will change your life."

— **Father Leszek Czelusniak,** the director of the Marian Formation Center "CANA" in Kibeho, Rwanda

"This is a remarkable story of how Rwanda, a country divided by ethnic hatred and shattered by one of history's bloodiest genocides, is reuniting and healing itself through a singular faith in the enduring love and forgiveness of the Virgin Mary. No matter what your race, religion, political affiliation, or personal belief system, you will be inspired by **Our Lady of Kibeho**—a true story of the power of faith and the great potential of forgiveness."

— **John Fund,** columnist for *The Wall Street Journal*

"Our Lady of Kibeho is calling the children of God from across the world to become her beautiful flowers in her garden of love. Immaculée, thank you sharing Our Lady's love with all of us in this beautiful book—you are truly an apostle of Our Lady of Kibeho! God bless you!"

— **Emerita Mukayiranga,** the founder of the Flowers of Mary in Kibeho Association

"**Our Lady of Kibeho** radiates with the enormous power of the Virgin Mary's love; a love so powerful it can change hearts and change the world. I urge you and those you love to read this book and discover how Our Lady's love can transform your life and bring you spiritual peace, happiness, and prosperity."

— **Steve McEveety,** producer of *The Passion of the Christ*

Our Lady

of

KIBEHO

Bro. Louis Mason, S.M.

Also by Immaculée Ilibagiza, with Steve Erwin

THE BOY WHO MET JESUS: Segatashya of Kibeho

LED BY FAITH: Rising from the Ashes of the Rwandan Genocide

LEFT TO TELL: Discovering God Amidst the Rwandan Holocaust
(also available in Spanish and as a 4-CD abridged audio book)

❁

Hay House Titles of Related Interest

YOU CAN HEAL YOUR LIFE, the movie, starring Louise Hay & Friends
(available as a 1-DVD program and an expanded 2-DVD set)
Watch the trailer at: **www.LouiseHayMovie.com**

THE SHIFT, the movie, starring Dr. Wayne W. Dyer
(available as a 1-DVD program and an expanded 2-DVD set)
Watch the trailer at: **www.DyerMovie.com**

❁

*CHANGE YOUR THOUGHTS—CHANGE YOUR LIFE:
Living the Wisdom of the Tao,* by Dr. Wayne W. Dyer

*COUNT YOUR BLESSINGS: The Healing Power
of Gratitude and Love,* by Dr. John F. Demartini

FATHER GOD: Co-creator to Mother God, by Sylvia Browne

*IF I CAN FORGIVE, SO CAN YOU: My Autobiography of How
I Overcame My Past and Healed My Life,* by Denise Linn

IN MY OWN WORDS: An Introduction to My Teachings and Philosophy,
by His Holiness The Dalai Lama; edited by Rajiv Mehrotra

MOTHER GOD: The Feminine Principle to Our Creator,
by Sylvia Browne

*PRACTICAL PRAYING: Using the Rosary
to Enhance Your Life,* by John Edward (book-with-CD)

PRAYER AND THE FIVE STAGES OF HEALING,
by Ron Roth, Ph.D., with Peter Occhiogrosso

❁

All of the above are available at your
local bookstore, or may be ordered by visiting:

Hay House USA: **www.hayhouse.com®**
Hay House Australia: **www.hayhouse.com.au**
Hay House UK: **www.hayhouse.co.uk**
Hay House South Africa: **www.hayhouse.co.za**
Hay House India: **www.hayhouse.co.in**

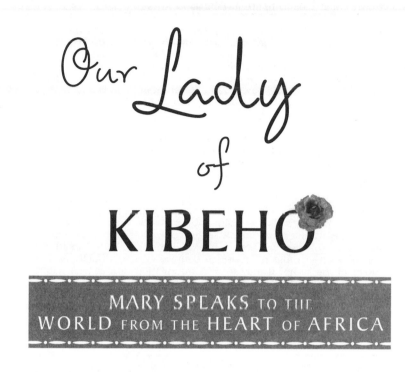

Our Lady of KIBEHO

MARY SPEAKS TO THE WORLD FROM THE HEART OF AFRICA

IMMACULÉE ILIBAGIZA

with Steve Erwin

HAY HOUSE, INC.
Carlsbad, California • New York City
London • Sydney • Johannesburg
Vancouver • Hong Kong • New Delhi

Copyright © 2008 by Immaculée Ilibagiza

Published and distributed in the United States by: Hay House, Inc.: www
.hayhouse.com • *Published and distributed in Australia by:* Hay House
Australia Pty. Ltd.: www.hayhouse.com.au • *Published and distributed
in the United Kingdom by: Hay House UK, Ltd.:* www.hayhouse.co.uk •
*Published and distributed in the Republic of South Africa by: Hay House
SA (Pty), Ltd.:* www.hayhouse.co.za • *Distributed in Canada by:* Raincoast
Books: www.raincoast.com • *Published in India by:* Hay House Publishers
India: www.hayhouse.co.in

Editorial supervision: Jill Kramer • *Design:* Tricia Breidenthal
Illustration of Mother Mary on p.186: Jami Goddess
*All photos appearing in this book are property of the author or have been
generously provided by the CANA Center in Kibeho*

All rights reserved. No part of this book may be reproduced
by any mechanical, photographic, or electronic process, or in the
form of a phonographic recording; nor may it be stored in a retrieval
system, transmitted, or otherwise be copied for public or private
use—other than for "fair use" as brief quotations embodied in articles
and reviews—without prior written permission of the publisher. The
intent of the author is only to offer information of a general nature
to help you in your quest for emotional and spiritual well-being. In
the event you use any of the information in this book for yourself, the
author and the publisher assume no responsibility for your actions.

Library of Congress Cataloging-in-Publication Data

Ilibagiza, Immaculée.
Our Lady of Kibeho : Mary speaks to the world from the heart of
Africa / Immaculée Ilibagiza with Steve Erwin. -- 1st ed.
 p. cm.
ISBN 978-1-4019-2378-5 (hardcover : alk. paper) 1. Mary, Blessed
Virgin, Saint--Apparitions and miracles--Rwanda--Kibeho. 2. Kibeho
(Rwanda)--Religious life and customs. 3. Catholic Church--Rwanda.
I. Erwin, Steve. II. Title.
 BT660.K52I45 2008
 232.91'70967571--dc22
                                                    2008034196

ISBN: 978-1-4019-2743-1

21 20 19 18 17 16 15 14 13 12
1st edition, November 2008

Printed in the United States of America

The statue of Our Lady of Kibeho that appears on the front cover of this book was
designed in 2001 by a team of Rwandan artists, who painstakingly attempted to capture Our
Lady's appearance based on eyewitness descriptions provided by the visionary Anathalie.
After seeing the first design that the artists came up with, Anathalie shook her head and said,
"That doesn't even come close to capturing Mary's beauty!" The visionary sent the artists
back to the drawing board 14 times before, in frustration, she realized that it was impossible
for any one mortal to capture the beauty of the Blessed Virgin. In the end, Anathalie told the
artists to do their best; today, she is very happy with the statue they produced because it was
created through love for Mary and radiates the Virgin's grace.

In all the writings and/or recorded interviews of visionaries throughout the ages, each
and every one has said that not a single picture or statue has even remotely reflected the true
beauty of the Blessed Mother.

To our most tender, patient, devoted, and merciful mother—the brightest and most beautiful star in heaven—Our Lady of Kibeho.

Thank you for being ever present in my life; for your endless tears of love; for your unyielding perseverance to save us from darkness; for your kindness; and for the gentleness of your constant beckoning that summons your children to follow you into truth, peace, and the glorious light of God.

Thank you from the bottom of my soul for being my mother, for being mother to us all, for being the true Mother of the Word. I shall love you eternally.

CONTENTS

Hail Mary, full of grace, the Lord is with thee;
blessed art thou among women, and
blessed is the fruit of thy womb, Jesus.
Holy Mary, Mother of God, pray for us sinners,
now and at the hour of our death.
Amen.

— THE HAIL MARY

FOREWORD

When God speaks of power, it is never in terms that the world understands, yet it is indisputable in terms of truth. The Blessed Virgin Mary, the mother of Jesus, is more known throughout the world; more revered by millions of people; and has had more buildings, paintings, statues, and other related images erected in her honor than any other person throughout time (outside of her son, of course, who is the meaning of her very existence).

In stark contrast to worldly money, power, and fame—which are fleeting moments, quickly forgotten and erased—Our Lady truly, and for all time, embodies and illuminates the eternal power of God. She lives as a daily reminder and indicator that her son, Jesus, never changes. He is the "light of the world" in a world that has lost its ability to see clearly. As I accidentally, or maybe providentially, bumped into my friend Immaculée Ilibagiza in front of Jesus's tomb in Jerusalem, I was reminded of this eternal truth as we spent the day walking in Christ's footsteps.

In *Our Lady of Kibeho,* Immaculée speaks in the only way she knows how: direct truthfulness. In her candid and honest approach that so many readers have already connected with and embraced, Immaculée once again writes magnificently with both truth and love about the appearances of the Virgin Mary in the village of Kibeho that began in 1981.

As you read through the different accounts of the visionaries, you cannot help but be compelled, as Immaculée surely has, to be drawn into Our Lady's immense love for each and every one of us. Immaculée's intense and personal journey with Mary, the mother of God, before, during, and in the aftermath of the Rwandan genocide has truly left an indelible mark of love on her soul for the mother of God and the gift of the rosary. May the words that await you likewise bring you God's peace, forgiveness, and unconditional love through the transcended light of His Blessed Mother!

— **Jim Caviezel**
(The actor who portrayed Jesus Christ
in the movie *The Passion of the Christ*)

INTRODUCTION

Show Us a Miracle

"Show us a miracle! Make us believe!"

Thousands of pleading voices poured out of the crackly speaker of the tape recorder belonging to our priest, Father Apollinaire Rwagema.

Father Rwagema had invited all the kids in the village to come to his little chapel after the regular Wednesday children's Mass. He told us he had a big surprise for us, and more than 200 kids showed up expecting some kind of treat. Father Rwagema didn't let us down.

We listened to every shout and every cheer. Some of us were fascinated by what the voices on the tape were saying, while others were intrigued because we'd never seen a tape recorder before, which sat on a wooden table in the center of the chapel's one small room. We gathered in a semicircle around that table, watching Father Rwagema press the PAUSE and PLAY buttons with his right hand while waving his left hand in the air for emphasis. He looked like a maestro conducting an orchestra.

"Listen closely to this part, kids," he said, gesturing to the tape recorder.

"We want to see a miracle!" the voices called again and again. We were all riveted by the bizarre demands the crowd was making, yet no one could have been paying closer attention than I was.

Father Rwagema switched off the tape player; he now had us as a captive audience and was ready to set the scene.

"What you're hearing is the sound of 15,000 people, some from this very village, pressed together in front of a wooden podium and calling out for a young man to make his appearance. They had been waiting for an hour to hear him talk, but they weren't really interested in what *he* was going to say—because they'd come to listen to Jesus!" Father Rwagema declared this with the flaring emphasis of an impassioned preacher, which is exactly what he was.

He turned the tape recorder back on, and the cheering crowd called one more time for a miracle before falling completely silent. All we could hear was the hissing of the cassette turning in the machine.

Then a young man began to speak in a gentle, reverent voice. "Yes, Lord, I have told them many times," he said. "No, Lord, they don't listen . . . they always tell me they want a miracle. They won't believe that you're talking to me, Jesus . . . not without seeing a miracle or a sign." He paused, as though waiting for a response, then added, "Yes, I will tell them what you say—"

Before the young man could finish his sentence, an enormous thunderclap erupted from the tape recorder so violently that the table wobbled. The room was charged with the tingling kind of current I felt when my brothers dared me to put my tongue on a transistor radio's battery.

Every kid in the room was transfixed by the thunder raging through the machine's speaker, as well as by the expression etched on Father Rwagema's face. His eyes burned with fervor; he looked up toward the ceiling as if he could see through the roof and into heaven.

A second violent peal of thunder rumbled from the machine, frightening the younger children, who began whimpering.

"That is the voice of God!" Father Rwagema proclaimed. "That thunder is our Lord Jesus Christ talking directly to us all, right here in Rwanda! Fifteen thousand people—many of your friends, neighbors, and parents—were there with me witnessing this miraculous event. It was a clear, blue day, but the thunder dropped from heaven like a hammer. Listen well, children, for I taped every moment to share with you . . . listen to his thunder!

"These many thousands wanted proof, and when God gave it to them, they were terrified. Many of them ran away, some fainted, and others fell to the ground and covered their ears or dropped to their knees crossing themselves. It was a miracle!"

The thunder ended as suddenly as it began. There was another brief silence on the tape before the crowd erupted once again, with some voices crying out in fear, and others shouting, "Praise Jesus!" They quieted down, however, when the young man resumed speaking.

"Jesus says you shouldn't be afraid, since he'd never do anything to harm his children," he told the crowd. "No one here has been injured, pregnant women needn't worry about their babies, and those with weak hearts will be well. . . . Yes, Lord, I'll tell them as you say . . . Jesus is telling me that he gave you thunder so you'd listen to his messages and not ask for miracles that have no meaning."

"Listen to this man, children," Father Rwagema urged us. "His name is Segatashya, and I met him last week after he spoke to Jesus. He is the newest of the visionaries God has chosen for the Virgin Mary and her son to speak to us through. It may be Segatashya's voice you're listening to, but his words come directly from Jesus."

"Our Lord says to stop asking for miracles," Segatashya continued on the tape, "because your lives *are* miracles. A true miracle is a child in the womb; a mother's love is a miracle; a forgiving heart is a miracle. Your lives are filled with miracles, but you're too distracted by material things to see them. Jesus tells you to open your ears to hear his messages and open your hearts to receive his love. Too many people have lost their way and walk the easy road that leads away from God. Jesus says to pray to his mother, and the Blessed Virgin Mary will lead you to God Almighty. The Lord has come to you with messages of love and the promise of eternal happiness, yet you ask for miracles instead. Stop looking to the sky for miracles. Open your heart to God; true miracles occur in the heart."

Father Rwagema switched off the tape and smiled broadly at the awestruck boys and girls looking up at him. I can still see that smile in my mind's eye 25 years later because it let me know that God *is* real.

In those days I saw that smile on many faces in Mataba, the rural village where I grew up in Rwanda, a small and unbelievably beautiful country in the heart of Africa. Sadly, it is not the beauty of the land most people think of when my country's name is mentioned; Rwanda is best known to the world for the bloody 1994 genocide in which more than a million innocent men, women, and children were savagely slaughtered, including the majority of my family.

But that day when I gathered with the other village kids to listen to Father Rwagema's tapes, the horror of the genocide was a dozen years away. If someone had told me then that almost all of my family and friends would soon be murdered in a holocaust, I would have thought them mad. My country was truly a peaceful paradise to me, especially during the early 1980s, when Rwanda's miraculous events inspired a national feeling of brotherly love and a renewal of belief and faith in God.

At that time, as incredible as it sounds, the Virgin Mary and her son, Jesus, began appearing to a group of young people in the southern Rwandan village of Kibeho. The visionaries brought messages from heaven intended for the entire world to hear: messages of love, along with instructions on how to live better lives and care for each other and pray more effectively. But with those messages also came dire, apocalyptic warnings that hatred and a thirst for sin would lead Rwanda and the rest of the world into a dark abyss. The Virgin Mary's prophecy of the 1994 genocide is one of the main reasons the Catholic Church has focused much attention on the apparitions in Kibeho.

In November 2001, the Church, in a very rare move, officially approved the apparitions of the Virgin Mary seen by three schoolgirls: Alphonsine, Anathalie, and Marie-Claire. The girls were tested and examined rigorously by doctors, scientists, psychiatrists, and theologians. Yet no testing could explain the miraculous and supernatural events that occurred when the Blessed Mother appeared to the girls. The evidence of a true apparition was irrefutable, and the local bishop said that there was no doubt a miracle had occurred in Rwanda. Thus, the Vatican endorsed what's known as "the Shrine of Our Lady of Sorrows," which is the only approved apparition site in Africa.

To date, the Church has only acknowledged what Alphonsine, Anathalie, and Marie-Claire witnessed, which took place between 1981 and 1989. However, several other visionaries saw both the Virgin Mother and Jesus (including Segatashya, whom I've already introduced), and they were also studied by the same team of investigators. Tens of thousands of onlookers—many of them priests and people of science—witnessed the apparitions of at least five of these other visionaries. While these apparitions have yet to be approved, the bishop in charge of these matters says that while the investigation is suspended for now, the book is not closed, so it's possible that more visionaries may receive Church approval in the future. In this book, I'll be focusing on the eight visionaries who were most popular and most studied.

I was actually among the earliest believers that Mary and Jesus had come to Rwanda. Long before Father Rwagema, our local priest, began traveling to Kibeho to tape the visionaries' messages, I knew in my heart that our country had been touched by a Divine power.

My parents frequently traveled to Kibeho and told me details of their visits, and I've always had great love for the Virgin Mary. This, coupled with my fascination with the apparitions, drove me to find out as much as I could about them so that I could share my findings with you in these pages. I met with the bishops, priests, and doctors who studied the apparitions; I've become friends with several of the visionaries themselves; and

I've repeatedly listened to the hundreds of hours of apparitions that Father Rwagema recorded. These are the sources I draw upon for this book. In other words, it's not a history lesson, but rather my personal account of an authentic miracle unfolding and the profound effect it had on my country, my parents, and my faith.

The shrine for Our Lady in Kibeho has become a place of worship and prayer for hundreds of thousands of pilgrims from across Africa, many of whom claimed miraculous healings at the site, yet most of the world hasn't even heard about this blessed place. It is my deepest hope that this small volume will help change that, and that Kibeho will become as well known as Fátima or Lourdes. The messages Jesus and Mary brought forth at Kibeho are of love—which today's world so desperately needs to hear.

❁ ❁ ❁

Chapter 1

My Faith
Was Born in Fátima

It's a difficult confession for me, but if it hadn't been for the apparitions of the Blessed Mother and Jesus at Kibeho, I may never have fully believed in God.

That may come as a surprise to anyone familiar with my first two books, *Left to Tell* and *Led by Faith,* which detailed how I grew up in a devout Catholic family, loved to spend hours in prayer, and adored the Virgin Mary. I also faithfully attended Mass every Sunday with my parents, Leonard and Rose, and my three brothers: Aimable (the eldest), Damascene (who was a few years older than I was), and Vianney (the baby of the family). Finally, during the three months I spent in hiding during the 1994 genocide, I decided to dedicate the rest of my life to serving our Father.

You could say that He is a pretty big part of my life.

As a child I had a remarkable affinity for all things related to God, but when my rational, inquiring mind kicked in around age 11, doubts about His very existence started chipping away at the foundation of my faith. Before I reached puberty, I was already wondering if I might grow up to be a confirmed atheist.

This youthful crisis of faith came upon me not because I was a particularly precocious child, but because I spent so much time thinking about God. In fact, my earliest memories are rooted in devotion. My brothers used to joke that instead of "Mommy" or "Daddy," my first words were "Hail Mary!" This could well be true, since I can clearly recall my mother reciting the rosary while rocking me to sleep in her arms.

By the age of four I was completely enamored with God, Jesus, and the Virgin Mary. Once a month my father would bring home a Catholic periodical called *Hobe*, a little newspaper specifically published for children. The pages of *Hobe* were replete with exciting Bible stories highlighting the power of faith, miracles performed by Jesus, and adventurous tales of saints and apostles. It's likely I learned to read from my father and older brothers, who told me the *Hobe* stories over and over until I'd memorized all the words and what they meant. But it was the drawings in each issue that truly inspired me.

My favorite illustration was of a typical young girl from a Rwandan village—a very poor but very happy child—saying evening prayers. She was kneeling beside her bed of banana leaves, hands folded in prayer and clasping a carved rosary. As the candle on her night table cast a yellow halo around her head, she looked positively angelic. *That's the kind of little girl God loves,* I thought, and for years I tried to emulate her.

As the only girl in a family of four kids, I had certain privileges my brothers didn't, including my own bedroom, which was practically an unheard-of luxury in a rural village. I took advantage of my privacy, converting my room into a personal sanctuary of devotion. My night table had a candle just like the one in the *Hobe* drawing; and a Bible, a rosary, and a statuette of the Virgin Mary were neatly arranged next to it at all times. Every night after my brothers went to sleep and my parents had doused the house lamps, I'd slip out of bed, light my candle, and pray the rosary on my knees just like the girl in the *Hobe* picture.

While most kids I knew dragged their heels to Sunday Mass, I was the first into church to ensure that I got the closest seat to the priest, where I assumed I'd be that much closer to God. And when Mass let out, I headed off to seek adventures with Him.

One Sunday when I was five years old, my friend Patricia and I decided to travel to the edge of our known universe—the other side of the village—to see if we could spot God in the distance. When we reached our destination, which seemed like a full day's journey from our home but was really less than a mile, my friend and I knelt in the middle of the dirt road, pressed our hands together in front of us, and began reciting the Lord's Prayer. We believed that our piety would encourage the Almighty Father to come chat with us, but instead of hearing His majestic voice, we were startled by a raspy chuckling.

"What on earth are you children doing praying in the road in the middle of the day?" asked Lionel, a local shepherd passing by with half a dozen goats. Both Patricia and I had read a story in the most recent issue of *Hobe* that said children should never be embarrassed about praying to God, because if they were embarrassed for loving Him, He would in turn be embarrassed for loving them. So we squeezed our eyes shut and prayed even harder, ignoring Lionel and the goats that brushed by our arms. Lionel kept laughing, and we kept praying. But by the time we said "Amen," the shepherd had stopped his laughter. Instead, we heard him grumbling, "What is the world coming to when children are praying instead of playing?"

In my world, praying and playing overlapped. One of my favorite childhood games was one I invented, called "Pictures in Heaven." Whenever a meteor shower lit up our village, which was often in the summer months, I'd bang on the doors of a dozen kids and gather them together in one of my dad's bean fields. I'd have everyone strike a pose toward the sky as the shooting stars streaked across the heavens.

"Those are flashbulbs on God's camera," I'd explain, pointing to the burning meteorites. "Pose nicely because God is taking our photographs and will show them to us when we meet Him in heaven!"

By my sixth birthday I had a reputation at home and in my village for being a very pious youngster, which delighted me because I was sure that both God and my parents were proud of my devotion. Yet there were occasions when my mother let me know I was taking Christian charity too far, like the time I gave away my brand-new shoes to a barefoot classmate on the first day of school.

"Immaculée, how could you give away those shoes? Do you know how much they cost?" she asked in exasperation. (Of course she couldn't get too angry with me, since she and my father, who were both teachers and made more money than most villagers, were known far and wide for doing charitable deeds.)

"Mom, I have to walk eight miles to get to school, but she has to walk nine miles. She needed the shoes more than I did," I answered.

"Well, the next time you feel an urge to give away shoes, give away your old ones," she said with a smile.

FOR MOST OF MY CHILDHOOD I WAS BLISSFULLY CONTENT with an unshakable faith in God. But about six months before I turned 11 years old, I inexplicably began to question everything I had, until that point, accepted as the gospel truth. Bible stories I'd never tired of hearing became an especially troubling source of unanswerable questions.

There is no way Jonah could live in a fish's stomach! It's not possible, I'd fret. Or my thoughts would turn on the priest as he shared scripture in church: *How does he know that Noah really built an ark and filled it with every animal—come on! As if cows and goats would last for 40 days and nights with lions and crocodiles on board! And as for what happened to Saul, well, the only ones there were him, his donkey, and God . . . and all of this happened more than 2,000 years ago!*

Suddenly everything I'd heard, been taught, and had put my blind faith in became suspect: *Is there really anything supernatural? Is there a heaven, or even a God? Is all of this stuff something adults invented to make children behave? Or something the Church made up so it can be powerful? How can I be sure who wrote the Bible? I can't! Who can prove that Jesus existed? No one can! Maybe these priests and pastors have been fooling everybody for centuries!*

If God and heaven don't exist, then what happens when we die? I'd wonder. *Are we just tossed into a hole in the ground, covered with dirt, and left in darkness for eternity? Does this mean I won't be with my family in heaven when we all pass away? And if that's the case, what's the point of living when there is so much sadness, sickness, and suffering in the world?*

It was all too much for my young mind to fathom, so I buried the dark thoughts as deeply as I could, trying to ignore the nascent depression I knew would swallow my heart if I accepted that God didn't exist. I began having nightmares that I was being hunted by devils and demons, and I'd wake up crying out for God to save me.

My parents, who had delighted in my faith, would have been devastated to know the doubts I was harboring, so I hid my turmoil from them. I went to church with my family and said prayers at night, but Mass seemed hollow and my prayers lacked conviction— neither brought me any comfort or reassurance. The air seemed to have been sucked out of my world. To many, the religious doubts of an 11-year-old may seem insignificant and of little consequence, but God and prayer were such an integral part of my being that losing them left me lost and vulnerable. As I pondered a world where no God existed, all I could envision was a hard and meaningless life.

God must have felt my anguish, for He found a way to dispel my doubts before they became too deeply rooted.

A few weeks after my crisis of faith began, one of my favorite teachers gathered the students around her desk to read us a story: it was about the apparitions at Fátima, and it changed my life forever. I'd never heard the word *apparition* before, and I had no idea that what I was about to hear would be of enormous significance to me.

"This is the story about the Virgin Mary coming to Earth and talking to three children, two girls and a little boy, who were shepherds in the mountains," Miss Odette began.

Despite my severe bout of religious skepticism, I still loved the idea of a mother in heaven watching over us, and I perked up at the mention of the Blessed Virgin. My teacher launched into what I thought was a beautiful fairy tale:

> The children were Lucia dos Santos, who was ten years old, and her younger first cousins, nine-year-old Francisco Marto and his sister, Jacinta, who was just seven. It was a beautiful spring day, and the children were watching over their sheep. They decided to say their rosaries as they'd been taught to do by their parents, but when they knelt to say their prayers, they grew frightened by a sudden flash of light in the sky. Afraid of being struck by lightning, they ran to the shelter of a big tree. When they looked up to see if a storm was coming, they saw a beautiful lady hovering in a glowing circle of light in front of them. The lady was wearing a flowing white dress and held a rosary in her hands, which were folded together in prayer.
>
> Lucia, Francisco, and Jacinta were very afraid, but the lady spoke to them in a soft voice that sounded like music: "Don't be afraid of me, dear children. I will never hurt you," she said.
>
> "Where are you from, your excellency?" Lucia asked, sensing that she was in the presence of greatness. Her fear left her completely, and she was overwhelmed with a sense of deep love.
>
> "I am from heaven, and I've been sent here by God Almighty," the lady answered gently.

I hung on every word, thinking, *Wow, what a beautiful story. I wonder who made it up? I wish something like that would happen to me; then I'd know for sure that God was real, and praying would feel good again.*

Miss Odette continued the tale:

"What do you want from us, your excellency?" Lucia asked, now realizing that she was speaking with the Virgin Mary. The lady said she wanted the children to come see her on the same day every month for six months, on this very same spot. Lucia promised that they would, and asked the lady if she'd join her in heaven one day.

"Oh yes," answered the lady.

"And my cousin Jacinta—will she go to heaven?" Lucia asked.

"Oh yes," answered the lady.

"And my cousin Francisco—will he also go to heaven?"

"Yes, he will, but he'll have to say many rosaries first," the lady answered sweetly. She then told the children that she'd soon take Jacinta and Francisco to heaven, but Lucia had work to do on Earth and would have to wait to go to paradise.

The lady came back every month as promised. During her many visits, she asked if the three children would be willing to endure suffering for God, as Jesus had, to make up for the world's many sins.

"Will you suffer as an act of reparation and for the conversion of sinners?" she inquired, and the children all promised her that they would.

News of the visions spread quickly throughout the mountains and to lands far away. At first the children were mocked and called liars, even by their own families, but soon all those who doubted them came to believe—70,000 people even journeyed to the mountains to witness their final visit with the lady. Although the Blessed Mother appeared only to Lucia, Francisco, and Jacinta, thousands who were watching the young seers witnessed many miracles during the apparitions, such as the sun dancing in the sky, the image of religious figures in the clouds, and miraculous healings.

Mary always told the children that she loved them very, very much, and pleaded with them to pray the rosary because it was the best way to protect against evil and assure a place in heaven.

"Isn't that a beautiful story?" Miss Odette asked the class.

It's the most beautiful story I've ever heard, I thought.

"What happened to the three children who saw Mary?" asked my classmate Miriam.

"Well," our teacher replied, "just as the lady promised she would, she took Jacinta and Francisco to heaven while they were still children. But Lucia is still alive today and has been doing great works for the Blessed Virgin for many years."

"What?!" I shouted, jumping to my feet. "What do you mean Lucia is still alive today? That was just a story you told, right, Miss Odette? It was just make-believe, wasn't it?"

"Oh no, Immaculée. All of that really happened exactly the way I told it to you," Miss Odette said, laughing at my stunned expression.

"No!"

"Yes," she insisted.

"How can that be, Miss Odette? How could the Virgin Mary come to Earth? How is it possible anyone could see her?"

"Well, it was a miracle."

"But I thought miracles only happened in the olden days, in Bible times, and that they only happened in the Holy Land."

"Oh no, Immaculée, miracles happen every day . . . God works them whenever and wherever He needs to. The miracle in Fátima happened in 1917, just 64 years ago. And Fátima is in a country called Portugal, which isn't as far away from Rwanda as it may sound."

"Miss Odette, are you fooling us?" I pressed her. "Did the Blessed Mother really visit those children?"

"Yes, she really did visit Lucia, Jacinta, and Francisco," she assured me patiently.

"And does the Church know about what happened?"

My teacher laughed again. "Of course the Church knows about it! The Church sent all sorts of priests and doctors to examine the children and make sure the miracles were really from heaven—they spent many, many years investigating to make absolutely sure it was all true."

"Then why haven't we heard about this? Why don't they talk about it at Mass?"

"Not everybody knows about apparitions, Immaculée, and not everybody believes in them. But Fátima isn't the only place Mary has visited children. She came to a young girl named Bernadette in a place called Lourdes . . . she's appeared to young people of faith before, and she'll do so to young people of faith in the future. Wherever Mary goes, she is remembered. Thousands of people still go to Fátima to visit the place where she spoke to the children. There they call her 'Our Lady of the Rosary' or 'Our Lady of Fátima,' and she is greatly loved."

My world brightened immensely, and my heart was free of the doubts that had plagued me for so many troubled weeks.

If the Virgin Mary is real, then Jesus is real, I reasoned. *And if Jesus is real, then God is real . . . and so is every word in the Bible!* Everything in my world had fallen right back into place.

As soon as I got home from school that afternoon, I shut myself away in my room, clasped my rosary, and prayed harder than I ever had in my young life, thanking God for letting me know that He truly existed and heard my prayers.

THE STORY OF FÁTIMA ENERGIZED ME SO MUCH I lay awake all night thinking about the three young visionaries and imagining what it must be like to encounter the Blessed Mother in person.

In my second book, *Led by Faith,* I wrote about how, after learning of the apparitions at Fátima, I devised an elaborate plan to entice the Virgin Mary to our village of Mataba. My friend Jeanette and I took her little brother, Fabrice, to the top of the low mountain where my father kept his goats. The three of us were almost exactly the same age as the children of Fátima, and among Dad's goats it was easy to pretend to be shepherds, just like Lucia, Jacinta, and Francisco had been. We prayed feverishly on the mountaintop for Mary to appear to us. To make Mataba a more inviting destination for her, we picked dozens of beautiful flowers and laid them in a huge circle around the hillside. Then we knelt in the center of the circle and prayed our rosaries. When the Holy Mother didn't come to us right away, we decided that we'd plant a sea of exotic blooms on the mountain that she couldn't resist coming to admire.

Jeanette and I were confident that the Blessed Virgin would come to us and entrust us with many important messages for humankind. We thought our fame would spread across Africa, and folks would travel for hundreds of miles to witness the miracle in Mataba. Thousands of people would surround our circle of flowers and watch the three young visionaries receive messages from the Queen of Heaven. Unfortunately, we lacked the power of our convictions. After a few weeks it was hard to convince Jeanette's brother to climb to the top of the mountain. When Fabrice did join us, he'd get frightened when the sun began to set and then beg us to take him home. We usually had time to say only one rosary before leaving, and we never got around to planting the Holy Mother's flowers. After a while Fabrice refused to come to the mountain at all, and Jeanette and I stopped going because we didn't have a third visionary as they'd had in Fátima.

But Mary did hear our prayers—we just weren't on the mountaintop when she arrived in Rwanda.

❦ ❦ ❦

Chapter 2

Mary Arrives in Rwanda

✿

Three weeks after Jeanette and I quit climbing the mountain to pray for the Virgin Mary to appear, my father arrived home from work and proclaimed in a loud voice that there had been a miracle in Rwanda.

"A miracle?! What is it, Dad?! What happened?!" I shouted, running to his side. "Tell me, tell me!"

"Don't you know that patience is a great virtue?" Dad asked me with a chuckle. "Anything worth having is worth waiting for, Immaculée, even miracles. So first we'll have our dinner as a family, and then I'll share my news with you, your mother, and your brothers during Igitaramo."

Igitaramo, an ancient and revered Rwandan custom for untold centuries, is a simple custom of homespun elegance. After finishing the evening meal, families gather around a large communal fire and sing songs commemorating our ancestors. Dancers in colorful dress entertain the villagers, and the most eloquent speakers relay news from other villages or tell old stories steeped in tribal legend. It's also a chance to gossip, settle disputes, tell jokes, and arrange marriages. Igitaramo has survived European colonization and remains a big part of Rwandan culture. (In fact, at this point Radio Rwanda broadcast a version of Igitaramo, which was filled with stories and songs, every night after 9 P.M.)

Our family didn't have a television or even a telephone, so our spare time was usually spent together. Dad particularly loved debating things during Igitaramo, so when he said that's when we'd discuss the miracle, I knew it was something he wanted us to look at closely.

As we were finishing dinner, he began telling us about how he'd visited Father Clement that day in our neighboring parish. Father Clement was the most revered priest in the region, as well as being a deeply pious, very well-educated, and wise man. He was also a good family friend—while he was especially close to my father, my brothers and I loved him so much that we called him Grandpa.

"A priest in Kibeho let Clement know about a 16-year-old girl named Alphonsine Mumureke, who says the Virgin Mary appeared to her at least five times in the past two weeks," Dad told us. "The girl claims that the Blessed Mother wants to be known in Rwanda as the 'Mother of the Word,' and that God Almighty sent her here with messages from heaven for the entire world to hear."

"Oh, I knew it, I knew it, *I knew it!*" I screamed, jumping up and dancing around the table. "She's real and she did come to see us!" Tears rolled down my face, and I was elated and heartbroken all at once. I was thankful that the Blessed Mother had come to Rwanda, but I was also kicking myself for abandoning my trips up the mountain: *We should have planted the flowers three weeks ago! Why didn't I keep praying? Mary should have appeared to Jeanette and me . . . clearly there's been a terrible mistake!*

My disappointment was short-lived, though, because I realized that my prayers had actually been answered. Mary loved me enough to come to Rwanda! What did it matter if she'd missed Mataba and landed in a different village? Rwanda was a small country I could just go to Kibeho, wherever that was, and see her there!

"Dad, did Alphonsine describe what Mary looked like? What was she wearing, and what else did she say? Where's Kibeho? Let's go there right now . . . I bet she's still there! We can finish eating supper in the car!" I sang out, pacing around the table.

"Sit down, Immaculée," Dad said with a laugh. "I don't have many more details except that she attends an all-girls Catholic school and that she goes into some kind of trance when the visions begin and is oblivious to everything around her. When it's over, she collapses into a sort of coma.

"But we're not going to Kibeho, so put that out of your mind right now. It's a long trip south of here in Gikongoro province, in a very remote spot that's extremely hard to get to. Even if I wanted to go there, which I don't, I'd never chance driving through the mountains on these roads at night. Besides, for all we know, this is just a wild story that a girl with an active imagination made up."

"But Father Clement wouldn't mention it if he didn't believe it was true, would he, Dad?" I asked.

"Immaculée's right, Leonard," my mother agreed.

Like my dad, Mom had immense respect for Father Clement and knew that if he voiced an opinion on something, it must be important. "Clement doesn't gossip or spread rumors; he only talks about things he's sure about," she added, giving my dad a curious, expectant glance.

"Well, that is true. Yet he told me this in confidence, and I'm annoyed with myself for bringing it up. It's just that I know how much Immaculée loves these stories, and I wanted to make her happy. Now she's *too* happy," he said, as I continued to skip around the room. He pointed to my chair, silently instructing me to sit down.

"I want everyone to be calm about this and listen to what I have to say," Dad continued. "Miracles can happen, but we make them happen through faith, prayer, and hard work. Aimable and Damascene are at the top of their classes in school because they worked hard and we prayed every night for them to be accepted into a good school. That's how to make miracles happen. We shouldn't expect the Virgin to appear out of thin air and hand us tuition for school, or for Jesus to write the boys' exams for them.

"Father Clement shared this with me because it is such an important issue and has the potential to do a lot of good or tremendous harm. Because I travel from school to school for my job, he's asked me to keep my ears open to what people are saying about this alleged apparition of Mary. Apparently, this Alphonsine girl has already caused quite a stir in her school, and a lot of nuns and teachers are upset. Who knows what this could be? The girl could be deranged or, God forbid, possessed by demons . . . the devil can work that way."

My father converted to Catholicism as a teenager partly because of his great love and devotion for the Virgin Mary, whom Protestants generally don't revere as much as Catholics do. So I would have thought that Dad would welcome news of a Marian appearance in Rwanda, but, like the Church itself, he was very suspicious of anything supernatural. Still, the possibility of the Blessed Mother appearing so close to home had fired up both his faith and intellectual curiosity. He'd worked himself into the mood for debate.

"So, what do you all think about this?" he asked now, pushing his plate toward the center of the table, indicating supper was over.

Everyone started talking at once, and the debate was on. My older brothers didn't believe a word of it, and I believed it all. (My younger brother was too little to understand what we were arguing about.) I exclaimed, "I've been praying for Mary to appear in Rwanda for weeks, and here she is! It must be true, it must be—I feel it in my heart!"

"Let's take this into the living room," Dad said, heading for his favorite chair. "It's time for Igitaramo."

My brothers and I were deep in argument as we entered the room.

"Immaculée, don't be so naïve," Aimable scoffed. "Like Dad said, it's probably a big, fat lie by some crazy kid who has no friends."

"If Mary was going to come to Rwanda, don't you think she'd go to Kigali, where there's at least a cathedral? I've never even heard of Kibeho before—nobody has!" Damascene added. "There's no way the Virgin would appear in a village no one even knows!"

"What about Fátima and Lourdes?!" I countered, leaving Damascene speechless for a moment.

"Please don't be taken in by this, Immaculée," Aimable said. "I know how much you love the Blessed Mother, but try to be realistic. This is probably another part of that anti-Catholic plot trying to make Mary look bad. You haven't forgotten about last year when they destroyed almost every statue of the Blessed Virgin in the country, have you? Even your favorite statue—gone, all gone! I bet this is the same kind of wickedness trying to turn people against Catholics and the Virgin." Aimable was visibly upset as he turned toward my father and added hotly, "Dad, someone should stop this before it gets out of hand. I mean someone should stop this *right now!*"

My eldest brother had brought up something that had been extremely hurtful to Catholics in Rwanda, especially to those like me who so loved Mary. There had just been an ugly, yearlong attack against the Blessed Mother across the country in which hundreds of statues of her had been smashed to bits, including the very beautiful one in our parish where I'd spent many peaceful hours in prayer. No one was sure who did it or why. Some say a rumor had been deliberately started that priests hoarded gold inside the statues; others claimed it was an extremist group of Protestants who considered the statues a form of idolatry that desecrated her image. But I think most people believed that it was the work of devil worshipers striking out at the mother of God.

"But maybe Mary has come to Rwanda *because* of what happened," I replied to Aimable. "She's come to show us that she's real! Maybe the devil knew she was coming and had all her images destroyed before she got here."

"Now you're talking like a little girl, Immaculée," my brother said dismissively. "This is a sick and silly joke; don't turn it into a war between heaven and hell."

"You kids were having a good debate," Dad jumped in. "But don't ignore your sister because she's only 11, Aimable. She's a smart girl, and she's making a valid argument. Remember, the Bible tells us that since Satan was cast from heaven there *has* been war between good and evil." Turning to me now, he urged, "Go ahead, Immaculée. I want to hear what you think."

It was the first time my father had asked for my opinion in a conversation, so I argued even more passionately: "I think Mary has come to Rwanda to remind us that her love brings us closer to Jesus. Maybe she's come because the devil came here before she did."

Aimable let out a long sigh and shook his head. "Well, I think it's a childish prank or an anti-Catholic plot. Either way, it's not a miracle," he retorted.

"Why would the Virgin ask to be called the Mother of the Word? It sounds too made up," Damascene noted.

"I've never heard that name before, and it does sound a bit made up," Dad agreed.

"What do you know about Alphonsine anyway, Dad? How old is she? Did she grow up in Kibeho?" Aimable asked.

"No, she's from a village in Kibungo."

"*Kibungo!*" Damascene and Aimable exclaimed in unison.

"That explains everything. Whatever's going on in Kibeho is definitely the devil's work," Damascene said.

Kibungo was a heavily forested province in eastern Rwanda and thought to be a center of pagan worship. It was said that voodoo and black magic were practiced there, and that Satanists lived deep in the jungle.

"Two kids at my school were from there," Damascene went on. "One night they woke up everyone in the dormitory screaming like they were being murdered. One of the priests tried to calm them, but they kept getting more frantic. Finally, he put rosaries around their necks and said a blessing while he sprinkled them with holy water.

"Those two boys went wild, shouting that the holy water was burning them. They ran outside, and we all chased after them. We watched them running in circles, and when they ripped off their rosaries, their feet burst into flames. We put a blanket on them to stop the fire. Only two things come out of Kibungo: devils and demons. And a pack of them followed Alphonsine all the way to Kibeho."

The story was so ridiculously unbelievable that I accused my brother of making it up.

"I swear that every word is true," he replied solemnly.

Damascene was an excellent storyteller and practical joker, but he never lied. "I wouldn't joke about someone being possessed by demons," he insisted. "I've never talked about this before because it scared me so much. A girl from Kibungo isn't seeing the Blessed Mary; she's seeing a demon who's tricking her."

Damascene had pretty much ended the debate. What could I say after a story like that?

Mom, who'd just finished her evening chores, walked into the room as Damascene was wrapping up his story. She saw the frightened look in the eyes of my little brother, Vianney, and scooped him into her arms.

"Leonard, why are you letting the children tell ghost stories?" she scolded my father. Then, turning to Damascene, she continued, "And you stop this talk of demons right now. Can't you see that you're scaring Vianney? It will be a miracle if we all don't have nightmares tonight. That's enough Igitaramo for this evening. It's best to just say your evening prayers now and go to sleep."

"Your mother's right," Dad said. "Let's not get too riled up about this. After all, I'm sure that the Church will get involved if Alphonsine keeps claiming to have visions. This is serious business, so let's say our prayers and ask God for guidance."

We knelt together in the living room, as we always did at bedtime, and prayed. I was certain that Mary had appeared to Alphonsine, so I made a special petition to her: *Thank you, Blessed Mother, for listening to my prayers and coming to Rwanda. If I can't get Dad to take me to Kibeho to see you, will you find a way to come to Mataba? Please make everyone as certain as I am that you're really here. I love you and hope to see you soon! Amen.*

Chapter 3

Mary Is Accepted

The Blessed Mother quickly answered my prayers.

It turned out that we weren't the only family debating Alphonsine's apparitions during Igitaramo. Within days the name Alphonsine Mumureke was on the lips of everyone in our village. The story of her apparitions had traveled overnight from tiny Kibeho to Rwanda's capital city, Kigali. People discussed her visions on Radio Rwanda, and it even made news in our neighboring countries of Burundi, Tanzania, Zaire (now the Democratic Republic of the Congo), and Uganda. Peasants around Kibeho were leaving their fields and milling about at the girls' school hoping to catch sight of the mother of God.

News of the Virgin's arrival had moved so quickly across the country that I considered it a miracle in itself. I'd asked Mary to make Rwandans believe that she'd arrived, and now the whole nation knew she'd come.

My father remained dubious, though. "This is what Father Clement was worried about," he said, when I asked him if we could now make a family trip to Kibeho. "People here are so poor that they're desperate for any kind of miracle to give them hope and ease the misery of daily life. But as we discussed last night, this is likely a hoax, a hallucination, or devilry."

"But everybody believes it's true, Dad, so why can't we go to Kibeho and see for ourselves?"

"Immaculée, everyone *doesn't* believe the visions to be true. Clement tells me that the priests, nuns, and students at her school are calling Alphonsine a liar and treating her very poorly. She could get herself expelled for something like this. Clement says Church authorities are looking into it, so until we hear what the Church has to say, let's assume that this girl is deluded or deceived."

This is exactly what happened to the children in the stories Miss Odette read to us about Fátima and Lourdes, I thought. I knew it was pointless to argue with my father—he was a wise and stubborn man, and my 11-year-old convictions weren't going to change his mind. I went to my room and got out my rosary, which I always thought of as a telephone cable that connected me to Mary. I knelt in front of her statue and prayed: *Dear Mother, next week is your son's birthday. Please give Rwandans a Christmas present. Let everyone be able to believe that the messages you are giving Alphonsine are true. Amen.*

The present I asked for didn't arrive for Christmas, but it made for a great birthday present! Dad gave it to me on January 12, 1982, just two days before I turned 12. He walked into the house, picked me up in his strong arms, and said, "Happy birthday, sweetheart. I think the Blessed Mother really has come to Rwanda!"

I squealed at the top of my lungs as my mother shook her head in amusement and muttered, "Here we go again."

Father Clement had just received word that a second student at Kibeho High School, 17-year-old Anathalie Mukamazimpaka, claimed to have been visited by the Virgin Mary in the dormitory. Anathalie was a devout and religious girl, and as Dad said, "The messages the two girls claim that they're receiving are similar in nature—very positive and in keeping with the Bible. They say that the Virgin wants us to be kind to each other, to think of Mary as our loving mother, and to pray the rosary every day in order to help bring us the love of her son. I'll admit that those are not demonic messages."

I pleaded with him to take me to Kibeho for my birthday, but he still refused. "Nothing's for certain yet," he explained. "Clement told me that the Church has an official procedure it follows when it investigates apparitions, so let's wait until the local bishop makes a ruling. Kibeho is in the archdiocese of Butare, Bishop Jean-Baptiste Gahamanyi's diocese. I know Gahamanyi; he's a good Christian and he's smart. If he decides that the visions are authentic, then maybe we'll take a drive to Kibeho if the roads aren't too bad. And I mean *maybe!*

"Keep praying your rosary and reading your Bible, Immaculée. If Mary wants you to go to Kibeho, it will happen. . . ."

IN MARCH THE VIRGIN MARY APPEARED to a third student at Kibeho High School: 21-year-old Marie-Claire Mukangango. Everyone in the village was talking about it, and news of yet another visionary was broadcast on the radio all day.

During Mass that Sunday Father Rwagema mentioned that after the rainy season in April and May, he was going to arrange a large pilgrimage to Kibeho so that parishioners could go listen to the Blessed Mother speak through the three visionaries. He said that he'd take his tape recorder and capture the messages for those unable to join them. Everyone in church now believed the apparitions to be authentic and was excited about making a pilgrimage.

After church our family crowded into Dad's little car to make the usual rounds of Sunday visits to relatives scattered all over the countryside. The trip to our many aunts and cousins took hours, and my brothers and I were already elbowing each other for room before our father turned onto the rutted goat path that served as our region's main road. During the drive, I asked him if what he'd heard at church convinced him that the apparitions were real. He took a long time to answer, and we knew he was about to pronounce his verdict on Kibeho.

"Well, I wasn't sure until I visited Father Clement yesterday and heard about the third visionary, Marie-Claire.

"Clement talked to a priest at the high school who didn't believe any of the girls' stories. He called them a pack of liars and wanted the three of them kicked out of school. But Marie-Claire approached the priest with a message she said had been given to her to pass along to him.

"'Excuse me, Father, I mean no disrespect,' she told him, 'but the Blessed Mother appeared to me today and told me to tell you that you've been unjustly tormenting her children and must do penance. She wants you to kneel down tonight, hold your arms open to God, and pray your rosary three times.'"

"Really, Dad? She gave him an order from the Virgin Mary?" Damascene broke in, clearly surprised. Both he and Aimable were studying at Catholic boarding schools and knew the consequences of being so insolent to a school priest.

"What did the priest say to Marie-Claire?" I asked, amazed that we were actually discussing a three-way conversation between a visionary, the Holy Mother, and a priest. *It's just like in the Bible when God told Moses to tell the Pharaoh to let his people go!* I thought.

"The priest called Marie-Claire a little liar and ordered her to stay in the dorm until morning, when he'd think of a proper punishment," our father replied. "But that night he decided to play it safe, just in case the visionaries were authentic, and because he didn't see any harm in some extra praying. So he locked himself in his room, drew the curtains so no one could see him, knelt on the floor, and spread his arms wide with the rosary, exactly as Marie-Claire said the Virgin had requested. Then when he finished, he put the rosary into his nightstand and placed some books and magazines on top of it before closing the drawer.

"The next morning the priest summoned Marie-Claire to his office to rebuke her once again. The student was smiling cheerfully when she arrived, and before he could speak, she said, 'Father, the Blessed Mother is very pleased that you prayed your rosary exactly as she asked you to, but she told me this morning that you shouldn't have piled all those books and magazines on the rosary when you put it back in your drawer. She says to keep it with you at all times and pray with it every day.'

"Father Clement told me that the priest's heart converted on the spot, and he's become a huge supporter of the visionaries. So to answer your question, Immaculée: yes, I do believe the Virgin Mary is appearing to these young girls in Kibeho. In fact, I'm so sure that I'm going to make the pilgrimage there with Father Rwagema and the others from our church."

"Oh! Can I go with you?" I begged.

"No, not this time. Look at the countryside out there," he said, nodding toward the sea of rolling hills stretching out endlessly before us. Some of the valleys below us were still dark in the midday sun. "We'll be making the pilgrimage on foot. That will show our devotion to Mary and honor the painful trek she made as she followed Jesus to Calvary. It's a journey of many days, and in some places there won't even be a road. We'll be sleeping in the bush and walking through the forest, and it's all far too dangerous for a young girl."

I pouted for a long while as the car bounced and lurched along. As I began to make a final appeal to my father, my mother, who had been sitting quietly in the front passenger seat, turned to face me. She saw the desperation in my eyes and smiled sweetly before ending the conversation. "The Holy Mother will hear your prayers just as clearly whether you're in your room or in Kibeho," she reminded me. "Don't ask again; the answer is *no*."

"Don't be upset, Immaculée," Dad said softly. "I keep telling you that one day you'll get to Kibeho. You just have to be patient."

I'd end up having to be patient for more than a decade before I'd walk the sacred ground of Kibeho. But since Father Rwagema made many pilgrimages and recorded them all, I was able to listen to the Blessed Virgin speak through the visionaries for hours and hours, week after week. The voices of the visionaries became so familiar to me that I felt as though I'd grown up with them, and eventually I knew their life stories as well as I did those of my own family. I've kept those stories like little treasures in my heart, and I share them with people whenever I can . . . like now.

Chapter 4

The First Visionary: Alphonsine

In the beginning, no one at Kibeho High School believed that the Virgin Mary had appeared to Alphonsine Mumureke. Not a single priest or nun, nor any of her classmates at the boarding school, accepted the 16-year-old's story that the Blessed Mother had come to her with messages that could save the world.

Why would they? There was nothing particularly special about the teenager to warrant a heaven-sent visitation. Alphonsine wasn't gifted academically (in fact, she often struggled with her grades), and although she was a good Catholic girl, she wasn't an expert on the Bible or particularly devout. She was a simple, dirt-poor peasant girl whose most remarkable achievement before November 28, 1981, was graduating from grade school and having the unbelievable luck of getting a chance at further education.

Alphonsine was born on March 21, 1965, and grew up in the tiny village of Zaza, a speck of a community in eastern Rwanda consisting of a few mud-brick huts, a one-room elementary school, and a little church. She was also the only Rwandan child I'd ever heard of who had grown up in a broken home. Divorce was extremely rare in our country, but Alphonsine's parents, Thaddee and Marie, had separated before their daughter was born. Marie dedicated herself to Alphonsine's welfare: despite crushing poverty and Rwanda's deep cultural and social prejudice toward single mothers, Marie kept food on the table and put her little girl through grade school. She worked from sunup to sundown, seven days a week, picking beans and gathering potatoes in the fields of local farmers.

Despite family woes and financial hardship, Alphonsine's childhood was a happy one. She loved to sing, and she mastered many of the nation's beautiful traditional dances as well. She attended Mass with her mother every Sunday and believed in God, even though she didn't read the Bible on her own or belong to any prayer groups like many of the other girls in Zaza did. But Alphonsine did love the Blessed Mother, and whenever she was lonely or had trouble with her schoolwork, she prayed to the Virgin for comfort and help.

It was assumed that after elementary school, Alphonsine would go to work in the fields alongside her mother. Poverty made high school an impossibility for the vast majority of Rwandan children, and Marie and Alphonsine were poorer than most. In rural Rwanda, the only career available for a single woman without at least a basic high school education was as a wife and mother— and coming from a broken home with no dowry reduced Alphonsine's chances of being selected as a bride.

But Marie had worked hard to ensure that her daughter had the requisites for high school and prayed for years that the Lord would bless her child with a higher education. Thankfully, a local priest who'd long admired Marie's faith and determination to provide for her daughter helped answer her prayers. The priest had friends in the school system, and when he learned that a space had unexpectedly opened up at the government-funded high school in Kibeho (about 120 miles from Zaza), he quickly arranged for the placement to go to Alphonsine. Since it was an all-girls Catholic boarding school run by nuns, Marie was confident that her daughter would be safe and taken care of there. Yet, although the government would be paying Alphonsine's tuition, it still took just about every penny Marie had saved for 16 years to cover her child's travel expenses.

Alphonsine's new school was actually among the poorest educational facilities in the country. Since there was no running water or electricity, the students had to spend a good part of their days fetching water from a distant stream, and they'd do homework by candlelight whenever the school's ancient generator broke down. Even so, for Alphonsine, being accepted here was like winning a full scholarship to Harvard.

It was the first time the girl had been away from home, and compared to what she was used to in Zaza, Kibeho seemed huge. Including herself, there were 120 girls in residence at the school, most of whom were Catholic, but there was also a handful of Protestants and even two Muslims. While Alphonsine was nervous and insecure in her new surroundings, she was able to make friends quickly thanks to her open and gregarious nature. She tried not to be too outgoing, though—in

Rwanda's conservative culture, children, especially girls, were expected to be quiet, well behaved, and demure.

Alphonsine studied hard, but she found it difficult to keep her grades up. She worried that if she failed her classes, she'd never find work to support herself or her impoverished mother. As she had since childhood, the girl prayed to the Virgin Mary for help . . . and she responded. What happened next forever changed the young lady's life, along with the lives of hundreds of thousands, or perhaps even millions, of others.

SATURDAY, NOVEMBER 28, 1981, began no differently than any other day. But moments after completing a pop quiz in geography, her last class of the morning, Alphonsine was overcome by a powerful rush of oddly mixed feelings. She was deliriously happy but also filled with dread. Confused and frightened, she stopped a friend in the hallway and described the upsetting emotions she was experiencing and confided that she thought she was losing her mind. Her friend laughed and told Alphonsine that she was just worried about how well she'd done on the geography test; she'd be fine in a few minutes when her nerves settled down.

Alphonsine agreed, took a few deep breaths, and felt better by the time she reached the dining hall, where it was her turn to serve lunch to the other girls.

Yet as she strolled from table to table filling her classmates' water glasses, the same sense of blissful contentment and almost paralyzing fear returned. She grew increasingly apprehensive, worrying that she'd missed an exam or an important appointment. Then she heard someone calling her name. She placed the water pitcher on a table and walked slowly toward the main corridor, where she felt she was being summoned. Her skin tingled and her hands trembled as she approached the foyer. She was also moving so strangely that she couldn't remember how to put one foot in front of the other. Within a few seconds, she didn't have control of her body at all.

The raucous schoolgirl chatter echoing through the lunchroom faded into silence. A gentle voice was speaking to Alphonsine, but it was unlike any she'd ever heard.

"My child," it beckoned, soft as air and sweeter than music.

Alphonsine lost all sense of time and space—she didn't know where she was or who was calling her. She hesitated, but then answered with the polite response Rwandan children use when addressing a respected elder: "Long life to you."

At this point, the teenager's line of vision narrowed so that all she could see was a brilliantly luminous white cloud materializing in midair a few feet in front of her.

"My child," the voice called to her again. Then, to Alphonsine's amazement, the most lovely woman she had ever beheld emerged from the cloud, floating between the floor and ceiling in a pool of shimmering light. She wore a flowing, seamless white dress with a white veil that covered her hair. Her hands were clasped in front of her in a gesture of prayer, her slender fingers pointing toward heaven.

The woman was barefoot, as an ordinary villager would be, but the complexion of her skin was flawless, so perfect in texture that Alphonsine couldn't determine its color. As the beautiful figure drifted toward the girl, her feet never touched the ground. Waves of love emanated from the majestic lady, embracing Alphonsine like the loving arms of a mother. The apprehension she'd felt moments before evaporated, and her heart filled with unimaginable joy. Sensing that she was in the presence of the Divine, she fell to her knees and asked, "Who are you?"

"I am the Mother of the Word."

"You are the Mother of the Word?" Alphonsine repeated. She didn't fully understand the meaning of the phrase, but she was now certain that she was kneeling before the mother of God. "My name is Alphonsine," she added happily, feeling surprisingly comfortable in the lady's presence, and blessed beyond belief that the Virgin Mary had chosen to speak with her.

"Of all the things in heaven, what makes you happy?"

"I love God, and I love His mother who gave us their son, Jesus, who has saved us!" Alphonsine immediately said.

"Really?" the lady replied, sounding very pleased with the teen's simple answer.

"Oh yes, truly."

"If that is true, then know I have heard your prayers and am here to console you. I want your friends and schoolmates to have your faith, for they do not have enough."

"Mother, if it's really you, and you've come to our school to tell us to have more faith, you must truly love us! It's such a great joy to see you with my own eyes!"

The Virgin asked Alphonsine to join the Legion of Mary, a Catholic group whose members dedicate their lives to live as the Holy Mother had—simply, humbly, and prayerfully, glorifying the name of God through their actions. Alphonsine agreed to do so right away.

Mary then stated that she wanted to be loved and trusted by people everywhere so that she could lead lost souls to salvation through Jesus. "Now watch as I return to heaven to be with my son," she said with a smile, ascending slowly upward and vanishing into the cloud's dwindling light.

Alphonsine toppled onto the floor, where she lay in semiconsciousness for more than ten minutes. When she opened her eyes, she saw the faces of her classmates peering down at her. Some were shaking her shoulders to try to rouse her, while others peppered her with questions about what had happened. After the sweet music of the beautiful lady's words, the schoolgirls' voices screeched in Alphonsine's ears, and she broke into tears realizing that she was no longer in the warm light of the Queen of Heaven. She tried to push herself to her feet, but she had no strength. All she could do was sprawl on the floor, disoriented and confused.

During her apparition, Alphonsine had been completely oblivious to her surroundings. Throughout the entire episode, her schoolmates had gawked in disbelief as she knelt on the floor, stared at the ceiling, and talked into thin air. At first she'd spoken in Kinyarwanda (the native language of Rwanda) and then switched to French, but then she ended up babbling in languages even the most educated of her teachers couldn't decipher, although some said there was some Hebrew and Latin in there.

Speaking to the Virgin Mary had drained Alphonsine of all her physical energy but left a residual joy in her heart. Her happiness bubbled out of her, and a smile crossed her lips as she gained fuller consciousness. "The Blessed Mother came to me," she finally said, gazing up from the floor. "The Blessed Mother spoke to me."

The students began taunting Alphonsine at once, even as she lay helpless on the floor.

The insults were led by Marie-Claire, one of the most outgoing and popular girls in school, who spat, "What a little liar! What are you playing at? What kind of game is our little Alphonsine trying to trick us with?"

"What were those noises you were making . . . were you having a fit?" asked another girl.

"Why would the Virgin speak to someone like you?" wondered another.

Still another classmate accused Alphonsine of trying to garner sympathy and pity because she came from a broken home. And then Marie-Claire suggested that Alphonsine had been performing a voodoo ritual she'd learned growing up in Kibungo, which all the students knew was rumored to be stalked by sorcerers and Satanists.

Finally, Sister Blandine pushed through the pack of girls circling Alphonsine and broke off their attack. The nun helped the dazed teenager to her feet and had to support her weight as they moved toward the office of the school director.

"Have I gone crazy, Sister?" Alphonsine asked.

"Let's see what the director and the nurse have to say," Sister Blandine replied.

The nun may have rescued Alphonsine from the other girls' inquisition, but the school director had many pointed questions of her own. She told Alphonsine that claiming to have a Divine visitation was a very serious matter in a Catholic school, bordering on blasphemy, and she demanded an explanation. The teenager wept in front of the director and said that she *couldn't* explain what had happened, since she didn't understand it herself.

"Then you're going to go back to the dormitory, stand in front of all the students and staff, and deny that you saw the Virgin. You will then pray for forgiveness," the director ordered.

Alphonsine dried her tears and said that her heart wouldn't allow her to deny what she'd seen: "All I can do is to tell you the truth. The Mother of the Word came to me; I spoke to the Virgin Mary."

The director sent Alphonsine to see the nurse, who found nothing physically wrong with the girl and sent her to her dorm room to rest. That evening the only thing the students were talking about was Alphonsine's "visitation." Some decided that she had a mental sickness; others said they knew her grades were very poor and suspected she was trying to win her teachers' sympathy before the Christmas exams. The worst gossip grew darker as it circulated around campus: Alphonsine had been possessed by demons in the Kibungo jungle before coming to Kibeho.

Alphonsine sadly realized that the most beautiful experience of her life had made her the target of scorn and suspicion. Nevertheless, in her prayers that night she thanked Mary for appearing to her and making her feel more loved than she had ever dreamed possible.

MARY APPEARED TO ALPHONSINE AGAIN THE VERY NEXT DAY. It was November 29, which happened to be the fourth Sunday before Christmas—Advent Sunday, which marks the official beginning of the Roman Catholic Church year and announces the approach of Christmas. The season of Advent not only celebrates Jesus's birth, but it's also meant to remind Christians to remain faithful because the son of God will return to Earth at the end of the world.

All of the students of Kibeho High School were at Mass listening to Bible readings encouraging them to be kind to each other and to cleanse their hearts and souls in preparation for the Second Coming. Yet as soon as it was over, Marie-Claire led a group of girls back to the dormitory to call Alphonsine a witch and demand to see some magic tricks. The pack was making other mean remarks when, all of a sudden, Alphonsine dropped to the floor as though she'd been shot.

She landed heavily on her knees and stared at the ceiling exactly as she had the day before. Her face lit up in ecstasy and she smiled peacefully, even as tears rolled down her cheeks. The transformation was so sudden and dramatic that some of the teasing students crossed themselves. But others hurled more cutting remarks at Alphonsine, who continued to smile and nod while looking upward, as though answering questions from someone she deeply loved.

Many of the girls howled with laughter, waving their hands in front of Alphonsine's eyes to break her fixed gaze. When she didn't react, Marie-Claire, who had acted in amateur theater, proclaimed her classmate to be the greatest actress in all of Rwanda. Her cronies snickered and shouted in Alphonsine's ears, but Alphonsine had no reaction to them. She couldn't react because she didn't know they were there—all she was aware of was the beautiful lady hovering about her again in the same glorious light.

"My child, I love you," the Virgin told Alphonsine in her soothing, lyrical voice. "Never be afraid of me; in fact, play with me! I love children who will play with me because it shows me their love and trust. Be as a little child with me, for I love to pet my children. No child should fear his or her mother, and I am your mother. You should never be afraid of me; you should always love me as I love you."

Mary again ascended to heaven, and Alphonsine dropped heavily to the floor. This second apparition was much shorter, but it took the girl just as long to emerge from the stupor that followed. She awoke to see Marie-Claire glaring down at her in disgust.

The Holy Mother continued to appear to Alphonsine in the school dormitory throughout December 1981, usually on Saturdays and in full view of the students and nuns. The verbal abuse and rejection grew more intense with each apparition, so the young woman avoided her schoolmates whenever she could, often going so far as to skip meals to avoid the glares in the lunchroom. Eventually a few students came to her in secret and begged her to tell them everything the Virgin had said.

"She loves us—that's what I feel the most when she's with me," Alphonsine shared. "Her love is so powerful that it could lift you up and carry you to heaven. When I see her, I can't see anything else; the rest of the world disappears, and there's just the lady and her beautiful light. Imagine how much your mom loves you, and then multiply that love a million times . . . the lady loves us even a million times more than that. She loves all the girls in the school and wants us all to love her. She doesn't want us to think of her as a strict teacher, but as a mom who really loves us and wants us to play with her.

"Because she loves us so much, she wants us to have more faith in God. During Advent we should reflect upon the return of Jesus. She told me that her son will return to Earth soon and that our souls must be prepared for his arrival. The world is in a very bad way, with a lot of hatred and sin, so she wants us to say the rosary every day to cleanse our hearts and show our love for her, for Jesus, and for God. She says that praying the rosary is the best way to show her our love."

"And what did she look like?" one of the girls asked breathlessly.

"She's always bathed in soft light and wearing a dress that must have been made by angels because it's completely seamless. Her skin shines like polished ivory, but it wasn't white like we see in pictures. She wasn't black either . . . she wasn't black *or* white. All I can say about her appearance is that she is more beautiful than anyone or anything on the planet; I don't have words to describe such beauty."

The girls were moved by Alphonsine and believed her story, but they were a tiny minority, and a silent one. They prayed for their friend to be believed by others, but they didn't come to her defense when she was attacked—that was too dangerous in such a hostile atmosphere.

What Alphonsine didn't share is that the Blessed Virgin was giving her important messages to deliver to government officials, even the Hutu president of the country, about their policies of discrimination against Tutsis and about letting Tutsis who'd been forced into exile return home. The teenager was told to deliver the messages with love—as well as to encourage the leaders to pray the rosary every day, to love their fellow humans, turn their hearts toward God's love, and follow the Lord's commandments.

Alphonsine had no idea how she was going to deliver the messages, considering that she had no money and no idea where to look for the president, except somewhere in the capital city of Kigali, where she'd never been before. She didn't need to worry, though, because the government would come to her in good time. In fact, in years to come Alphonsine would become known as the "holder of many secrets." But during the first months of visions, she was known as the teller of many lies, and she paid the price.

IRONICALLY, IN KINYARWANDA, ALPHONSINE'S LAST NAME means "leave her alone; she speaks the truth." But no one would leave her alone and, with a few exceptions, no one thought she was speaking the truth.

Some girls made a game of tossing rosaries at Alphonsine while she was on her knees during an apparition— the idea was to lasso her neck, much like the carnival game of tossing a ring around a soda bottle. Piles of rosaries landed in front of the visionary, but a few believers placed theirs respectfully before her, praying that Mary would bless their beads. Alphonsine's gaze never strayed from the Virgin during an apparition, so she didn't see anyone putting rosaries around her. When the Blessed Mother told Alphonsine to pick them up so that she could bless them, the girl reached into the pile blindly and managed to pick up only those that belonged to the faithful. The beads tossed by the mockers stuck to the ground like anchors.

The more Alphonsine spoke to Mary, the more familiar and comfortable she became in her presence. She chatted with the Queen of Heaven as breezily as if she were sitting at a kitchen table gossiping with a favorite aunt.

"Listen to the way she talks to her," Marie-Claire and others would say. "Would she use slang if she was really speaking with the Holy Mother? Who would call the

Virgin Mary 'sweetie' or 'darling'? That's the way you talk to a girlfriend, not the mother of God!"

When asked why she used such familiar terms with the Virgin, Alphonsine responded, "Because she wants us to talk to her like she's our mom, not like she's our principal or boss."

At the end of each apparition, Mary told Alphonsine when she'd appear to her next, and asked her to pass the information along. When word of the visions leaked into the village, local peasants scheduled their days around the apparition times and would hang around the school hoping to witness a visitation of the Holy Mother. Once the villagers heard about what was going on, the news jumped to the next village, and the alleged apparitions in Kibeho spread across Rwanda in days. The visitations were soon being hotly debated in every province, village, and family (including mine, as I've already mentioned).

All this attention infuriated the administration of Kibeho High School, as well as the local clergy, who thought that an attention-seeking teenager had turned the school and parish into a national laughingstock. They worried that the longer this carried on, the worse the embarrassment would be when the girl was exposed as a fraud. In an effort to silence Alphonsine, one of the priests even gave Marie-Claire the go-ahead to torment the visionary further. The older girl almost gleefully helped organize groups of students to physically abuse Alphonsine during her apparitions: they pulled her hair, twisted her fingers, pinched her skin as hard as they could, screamed into her ears, and shone a powerful flashlight into her open eyes. Alphonsine never blinked, winced, or flinched, no matter what they did. When she was in ecstasy, she was impervious to pain and unaware of her physical environment.

One day Marie-Claire held a burning candle under Alphonsine's right arm, which Alphonsine didn't react to. The Virgin had to ask her, "My child, do you know that they are burning your arm?" This is the one time Alphonsine reacted to a tormentor and pulled her arm away. But the Blessed Mother hadn't specified which arm was being burned, so Alphonsine pulled away her left one, giving Marie-Claire no satisfaction as she continued to hold a flame against the visionary's skin without results.

In mid-December the priest who assigned Marie-Claire the mission to expose Alphonsine stuck a needle several inches long deep into the young visionary's arm during an apparition, to no avail; Alphonsine just kept chatting happily with Mary.

During one visit, Alphonsine was heard to say, "Mother, they won't believe your messages because they think I'm crazy." Fearing that she'd been labeled a hopeless liar, the girl began praying for Mary to intercede on her behalf and appear to other schoolgirls as well. She hoped that if others saw the Holy Mother, then the school would believe that she'd been truthful all along. The half dozen or so girls who'd by then accepted Alphonsine as an authentic visionary knelt beside her in prayer, pleading with the Virgin to appear to another student.

As I've learned and said so often, prayers to Our Lady do not fall on deaf ears.

🌹 🌹 🌹

Chapter 5

The Second Visionary: Anathalie

There couldn't have been a more inspired choice for a second visionary than Anathalie Mukamazimpaka. The 17-year-old student fit the bill perfectly: she was from a large and devout Catholic family; she'd been a member of the Legion of Mary and other Catholic youth groups for many years; she'd read the Bible every day, as well as prayed the rosary every morning and evening; she'd never missed a Mass; and she was known to be one of the most pious students in school. If anyone could lift the cloud of suspicion from Alphonsine and prove that the Virgin Mary had really come to Rwanda, it would be Anathalie. Even her last name, which means "the person who settles arguments and brings peace," was perfectly suited for the job. And she got it.

On Tuesday, January 12, 1982, Mary made her first appearance to Anathalie around 7 P.M., shortly after the evening meal. Anathalie decided to go to the chapel to pray but, as had happened to Alphonsine, she became consumed by a storm of conflicting emotions—elation one moment, deep fright the next. She grew dizzy, and her body began to shake. Worried that she was going to faint, she returned to the dormitory and sat down on her bed. She began praying her rosary, hoping that the familiar practice would help calm her. Because Anathalie knew and recited the rosary so well, a few other girls joined her.

For a few moments, praying in unison with her friends calmed Anathalie. But then her heart started beating so loudly that she could no longer hear the words, and she was gripped by an inexplicable fear. Her hands trembled so violently that she couldn't move her fingers along the rosary beads, and her lips stopped moving. In astonishment, she realized that she'd forgotten the words to something she'd recited at least twice a day, every day, since childhood. She turned to her friends for help, but they were no longer there, and it had suddenly become very dark.

Anathalie shut her eyes and prayed that whatever was happening to her would stop. When she opened them again, she noted a blush of light on a distant horizon. It provided enough illumination for her to see she was no longer in the dormitory with the other girls, but standing in a meadow of oddly colored flowers and grass that stretched out endlessly before her. Thousands of transparent red circles floated in the air around her like little soap bubbles, bursting into soft explosions of crimson mist. The strange surroundings filled her with such confusion that she began to cry. Through her tears she saw a white sphere descending from above that emitted such an intense light she had to shield her eyes.

An unseen woman spoke to Anathalie from the light, and she sounded so forlorn that the girl thought her heart would break. "My child," the voice said, "I am sad because I have sent a message and no one will listen to my words as I desire." The anguish the woman expressed was so wrenching that it made Anathalie cry harder. Although she saw only the light, the girl was certain that the Blessed Mother was speaking to her, and her sorrow clawed at the girl's heart.

"It is my wish for you to cry as you do now," the voice explained. "Your tears are punishment—not because you have sinned against me, but to serve as a reminder that I can punish those who choose to ignore my messages. My child, you must pray, for the world is in a horrible way; people have turned from God and the love of my son, Jesus."

Mary then proceeded to map out what Anathalie's future would be if the young visionary volunteered to live her life in the service of the Lord: "So many souls are running to ruin that I need your help to turn them back to my son. As long as you are on Earth, you have to contribute to the salvation of souls. If you will work with me, I shall give you a mission to lead those lost souls back from the darkness. Because the world is bad, my child, you will suffer—so if you accept this mission, you must also accept all the sufferings I send you with joy, love, and patience."

The Holy Mother told Anathalie that, along with any pain she would endure, she must lead a life of mortification, too: a life of discipline, humility, prayer, and denial of the body and its appetites. "No one goes to heaven without suffering. And as a child of Mary, you may never put down the cross you bear," she stated.

"I accept, Mother," Anathalie replied through her tears. "I accept my mission willingly."

Then the Blessed Virgin told Anathalie what she'd told another messenger—Bernadette of Lourdes—many years earlier: "I cannot promise you happiness in this world, but I can promise you eternal happiness in the next world."

At the end of Anathalie's first vision of the Blessed Mother, Mary told her to find a copy of the book *The Imitation of Christ,* open it to a random page, and plant the first words she read deeply into her heart.

"Now I will leave you," the Virgin said. "But clasp your rosary tightly in your hand and kneel in order that I may bless you, my child." As Anathalie knelt, the light around her brightened and, for a fleeting moment, she saw the shadow of a woman standing in front of her and making the sign of the cross. Then darkness returned, and the schoolgirl was alone.

When Anathalie opened her eyes she felt weak and depleted. She was lying on her bed with her rosary dangling from her right hand, as a dozen of her friends and several nuns stood above her. They told her that she'd fallen into the same trancelike state Alphonsine had—but unlike that girl, when Anathalie claimed that she'd spoken with the Holy Mother, those who'd witnessed her ecstasy believed her at once. One of the nuns even knelt down before Anathalie and asked the young lady to bless her.

Anathalie's apparitions became as frequent as Alphonsine's, and after four or five of them, Anathalie not only heard Our Lady, but she also saw her in all her radiant beauty. When Anathalie later found *The Imitation of Christ,* written by the medieval monk Thomas à

Kempis, she opened it to a random page as Mary had instructed. The first passage she read said that "the things of this world are short-lived, but heaven's wealth is eternal."

Anathalie took this to be confirmation of what the Blessed Virgin had told her: that she must lead a life of suffering and self-sacrifice with a loving heart and constant patience. The mission Anathalie accepted that night is one she carried on for more than 25 years and continues to this day, as you shall see in the coming pages.

AFTER ANATHALIE'S FIRST APPARITION, the Holy Mother appeared to Alphonsine and instructed her to take Anathalie's hand and kneel with her in prayer, in order to help convince everyone that the Virgin was indeed visiting the two teenagers. And while many at the high school *were* convinced, plenty remained doubtful. The school director, who'd assumed Alphonsine was mentally ill, now worried that her school had become a target for the devil.

Marie-Claire, always Alphonsine's greatest detractor, declared war on Anathalie as well, accusing the two girls of forming a diabolical plot to gain national attention. She began spying on Anathalie and Alphonsine, reading their letters and diaries when they were away from the dorm, and watching them closely day and night for signs of collusion. Because of this, Alphonsine and Anathalie avoided each other so as to not draw suspicion or accusation. And while both girls continued to receive regular apparitions, they were always at different times.

Marie-Claire was so incensed by what was happening that she personally complained about the "false visionaries" to the head of the local archdiocese, Bishop

Jean-Baptiste Gahamanyi. When the bishop told the impetuous girl that he'd already spoken to Alphonsine and that the situation was being monitored, she only became angrier. She worked herself into such a state over the mischievous "scam" Alphonsine and Anathalie were perpetrating under the bishop's nose that she vowed not to rest until she'd unmasked their fakery. And if any student was in a position to debunk and humiliate the visionaries, it was Marie-Claire Mukangango.

Marie-Claire entered the world in 1961 in one of the poorest areas of southern Rwanda, and she was a born fighter. Her father died a few months after her birth and her mother often had difficulty providing for her, so Marie-Claire lived with her grandparents for much of her childhood. Perhaps because she had an unstable home life as a child, Marie-Claire learned to fend for herself early on and didn't let people push her around or take advantage of her. And she never felt sorry for herself; rather, she was independent, saucy, bright, charming, and charismatic. Raised Catholic, she believed in God, the saints, and all the sacraments that are part and parcel of a Catholic upbringing but wasn't very religious. Sitting in church was not her favorite pastime . . . in fact, she had a hard time sitting anywhere for any length of time. She was brimming with energy and grew fidgety and restless when kept indoors. She'd rather be running around a soccer field or out dancing—which she loved with a passion—than be stuck in a classroom or attending a prayer meeting with the other girls. Some even described her as a wild child.

Marie-Claire was indeed loudmouthed, obstinate, and often rude; however, she was also open and honest, which tended to make people trust her. And while she could be sharply critical of those who annoyed or offended her, her quick wit kept her friends laughing and in good spirits. She loved to talk and debate with friends, and she won most arguments she engaged in with the sheer force of her personality—if Marie-Claire was convinced she was right about something, no one could prove her wrong. Her self-confidence and outgoing nature made her popular, even admired. She was voted class president by her schoolmates year after year because they knew she'd always speak up for them and wasn't afraid to stand up to any of the teachers, nuns, and priests who ruled Rwanda's Catholic school system.

And she certainly wasn't afraid to stand up to Alphonsine and Anathalie, or anyone who supported their status as visionaries. Even though Marie-Claire wasn't very devout, she did pray to the Virgin Mary and was offended that anyone would be shameless enough to use the Holy Mother to win popularity and favor with others. She began praying the rosary to ask Mary to help her rid the school of the false prophets.

By early February, Marie-Claire's campaign of ridicule and harassment against the two young seers had become so nasty that even the priest who'd asked her to torment and discredit Alphonsine months earlier now cautioned the young woman not to be so mean. But Marie-Claire had a stubborn streak, so it would take more than a priest's scolding for her to look kindly upon Alphonsine and Anathalie.

It would take a miracle.

Chapter 6

And Then There Were Three: Marie-Claire

The miracle began on March 1, 1982, when Marie-Claire fainted during a walk in the garden between classes. A few minutes later she came to—or so she thought.

Instead of being outside in the sunshine, she was now in the dark with no idea where she was. The air stank with an odor of human waste and decaying flesh so disgusting she wanted to vomit. She got to her feet and ran blindly through the darkness, hoping that she was heading toward the school. She banged into the main door, and when she flung it open, the putrid stench disappeared and the daylight returned. She ran into the dormitory and found herself standing in front of Alphonsine, who was having an apparition and chatting amicably with the Holy Mother.

Marie-Claire looked down at her clothes and found that they were soaking wet. That's when she realized that two classmates were holding her up by her arms and walking her toward her bed. "Did I fall into the stream?" she asked, thinking she must have bashed her head and hallucinated.

The girls gave their friend a queer look and told her they'd found her lying semiconscious in the school chapel. They tried to get her to return to the dorm, but she refused to leave, mumbling that she'd never again set foot in the room where the visionaries had their apparitions. The two girls ran for help and returned with a nun who carried a large bottle of holy water brought from Lourdes. After the nun doused Marie-Claire with the water and said a benediction over her, the girls carried their friend to her room.

Marie-Claire had no idea what had happened except that she'd been unconscious for a good part of the afternoon. She had no answers to offer the many girls who passed by her bed asking about her experience. She was so shaken that evening that she began writing a letter to her mother, saying she'd taken ill and wanted to come home to rest for a while. But she'd only written a few words when she again lost consciousness and was back in the dark, but this time she wasn't alone—two menacing figures approached her from the shadows. Marie-Claire couldn't clearly identify who was standing in front of her, but they hovered in the darkness like specters. When they spoke, their wheezing voices were threatening.

"More of us were supposed to come for you tonight, but they haven't arrived," said one.

"But we'll be back. We're never far away," said the other, and then they both vanished. Marie-Claire rubbed her eyes, only to discover that she was on the floor of the school chapel surrounded by classmates, including Alphonsine, who handed her a little statue of Our Lady of Lourdes.

"Keep her with you to protect you from the evil one," Alphonsine said. "Last night when the Blessed Mother appeared to me, she warned me that the devil was planning to attack students at the school. She says that we can protect ourselves from the enemy by wearing our rosaries."

Marie-Claire stared at Alphonsine but didn't say anything.

"I will pray for you," Alphonsine added as she left the chapel.

"I don't need prayers from *her*," Marie-Claire told the other girls, and then asked them how she ended up in the chapel again.

They told their friend that she'd dropped her pencil while writing, and when she bent down to retrieve it, she'd fallen off the bed and had a fit or seizure—her body had flailed about wildly, her eyes rolled back into her head, and her tongue hung out of her mouth. The girls had tried to help but could do nothing, and when the fit ended, she'd run to the chapel and collapsed.

Marie-Claire shook her head in disbelief and looked down at the statue Alphonsine had given her. "All of this is the fault of those phony visionaries. I told you they'd bring us trouble. If demons are haunting this school, it's because of Alphonsine's voodoo!" she replied angrily.

The next morning, March 2, the girls were in their religious studies class learning about the Holy Mother's appearances to the children of Fátima. As part of the lesson, the nun—one of the few members of the faculty who believed Alphonsine and Anathalie to be true visionaries—instructed the girls to sing the hymn "In Fátima's Cove."

All Rwandan girls love singing, and singing in class, especially about the Holy Mother, could be a real treat. The young ladies jumped to their feet, clapping their hands and stamping their feet to bring energy and life to the old hymn:

> *In Fátima's cove on the thirteenth of May,*
> *the Virgin Maria appeared at midday.*
> *The Virgin Maria surrounded by light,*
> *God's mother is ours for she gives us this sight.*
> *The world was then suffering from war, plague, and strife,*
> *and Portugal mourned for her great loss of life.*
> *To three shepherd children the Virgin then spoke,*
> *a message so hopeful, with peace for all folk.*
> *With a sweet mother's pleading, she asked us to pray,*
> *do penance, be modest, the rosary each day.*

Halfway through the song, Anathalie told the nun that her skin was tingling, which was a sign the Blessed Mother was about to appear to her. She asked permission to go to the chapel, which the nun immediately granted, telling the rest of the girls to go with their schoolmate and keep singing the entire way.

Marie-Claire, who sat behind Anathalie in class, followed reluctantly at the back of the line. She thought that the nun was out of line and hated seeing the visionaries being encouraged. And as soon as they entered the close quarters of the small chapel, the young woman became very uncomfortable as the panic and fear of the previous day's blackouts rushed back to her. She bolted for the door but lost consciousness before making it outside. As she'd already done twice within 24 hours, she opened her eyes and found herself somewhere she didn't recognize. This time she wasn't in the dark, though—she was standing beneath a rainbow-colored sky in an open field of perfectly manicured grass. Each blade bent from the weight of fat drops of dew that caught colors of the sky like a million crystal prisms.

Marie-Claire caught her breath. It was the prettiest thing she'd ever seen, but the beauty didn't calm her down. She could think of two explanations for what was happening to her, and neither was good: either she was going insane, or the devil had taken possession of her senses. Then, out of nowhere, a soft voice called out her last name.

"Mukangango."

Marie-Claire spun around, her fists clenched and poised in front of her like a boxer. She thought that the specters who'd accosted her the previous night had returned to finish her off. She looked around in every direction but only saw the endless sea of shimmering grass. She responded wordlessly to the voice by raising her fists higher and planting her feet firmly on the grass.

"Mukangango," the voice called again.

No one had ever said Marie-Claire's name so sweetly. The tender voice, like that of a loving mother, was as soothing as a lullaby. But the girl was distrustful and answered the voice with a challenge: "Okay, you've found me. I am Mukangango. I'm here, and I'm ready to fight!"

With an affectionate laugh, the voice asked, "Why would you want to fight me, my child? What is making you so afraid? Never be afraid of your mother!"

At that moment, Marie-Claire realized with certainty that it was the Holy Mother who was speaking to her.

"I thought the devils who haunted me in the night had returned to take me away," she admitted.

"Oh no, my poor child," Mary said reassuringly. "There is no need to be afraid of them. I promise the things of the night that threatened you will not frighten you again."

The Blessed Mother then asked Marie-Claire to sing a song for her using words Jesus spoke during his Sermon on the Mount: "Blessed are those who are persecuted because of righteousness, for theirs is the kingdom of heaven. Blessed are you when people insult you, persecute you, and falsely say all kinds of evil against you because of me."

The words made Marie-Claire feel ashamed because they described her treatment of Alphonsine and Anathalie to a tee. She'd insulted and persecuted the visionaries for doing what Mary had told them to do: encouraging people to give their hearts to Jesus.

"Please child, sing the song for me," the Virgin requested again.

"No, I won't," Marie-Claire replied. "I-I don't have a good singing voice."

"Then I will ask your sister to sing with you," Mary said, sounding amused at the young woman's excuse.

Suddenly Marie-Claire saw Anathalie beside her, looking up at Mary. Marie-Claire followed Anathalie's gaze but couldn't see Our Lady. However, she could still hear her beautiful voice: "Sing this song with your sister."

"Yes, Mother," Anathalie agreed with a smile. She took Marie-Claire's hand in hers, and together they sang to the Virgin.

As the song ended, Mary said farewell to the girls, and Marie-Claire realized that she was lying on the chapel floor again, too exhausted to say anything to the classmates who were looking down at her in disbelief.

NONE OF THE STUDENTS OR STAFF PRESENT at Kibeho High School on March 2, 1982, ever forgot the atmosphere on campus that night. Word spread in a matter of minutes that Marie-Claire, the sworn enemy and most outspoken critic of the school's two visionaries, had confessed she'd been visited by the Holy Mother, too.

Thirty students described watching Marie-Claire enter a state of ecstasy in the school chapel, hold hands with the visionary Anathalie, and sing to the Blessed Virgin. She then collapsed on the floor in such a mental fog that she had to be carried to her bed. The story was told a hundred times by each of the 30 witnesses, each time from a different perspective and with slight variations of the details. But every version had an identical central theme: the Marie-Claire who'd walked into the chapel that morning was not the same Marie-Claire who'd been carried out.

The young woman was in a constant state of prayer after her apparition, kneeling for hours and praying the rosary, begging the Holy Mother for forgiveness. She recanted every accusation she'd made about Alphonsine and Anathalie and swore that she'd devote her life to serving God. Her rude, brusque, and aggressive manner had essentially vanished overnight, and, as passing years would prove, would never return. Marie-Claire was a perfect example of the spiritual conversion the Blessed Mother had been calling for since first appearing to Alphonsine. No, Marie-Claire wasn't an incorrigible sinner, but like so many Rwandans (and like so many people everywhere in the world), she'd been too preoccupied with the distractions of life to focus on the spiritual needs of the soul. Miracles had been happening in front of the girl for months, but she'd been so preoccupied with exposing lies that she'd missed the truth.

Later, she said that life would have been much easier and more spiritually rewarding for her if, instead of channeling her energy and time to discredit Alphonsine and Anathalie, she'd stopped for a moment and really *listened* to the messages. After one apparition, Marie-Claire commented that one of Our Lady's greatest sorrows during her many visits to Kibeho was that not enough people truly listened to the loving advice and counsel she offered through her visionaries. Too many individuals came to the village simply to witness a miracle, and while their eyes and ears searched the heavens for a supernatural event, their hearts failed to hear the messages Mary repeated again and again: love God, love and be kind to each other, read the Bible, follow God's commandments, accept the love of Christ, repent for sins, be humble, seek and offer forgiveness, and live the gift of your life how God wants you to—with a clean and open heart and a clear conscience.

After the first visit to Marie-Claire, during which she could only hear the Virgin, the Blessed Mother began appearing to the novice visionary many times a week. When Marie-Claire actually saw her, she said that Mary descended to her from heaven on a soft, silver cloud. Like Alphonsine, Marie-Claire claimed that the Queen of Heaven was a young woman who exuded warm, motherly love; that her skin was neither white nor black; and that she was wearing a seamless white dress with a white veil covering her hair.

Marie-Claire further shared that the lady was carrying a black rosary unlike any she'd seen before, which the mother of God told her was an ancient one called "the Rosary of the Seven Sorrows." The rosary held deep meaning for Mary, who said that she'd soon teach Marie-Claire how to pray this special rosary, and that it would be the girl's mission in life to reintroduce it to the world. Just like Anathalie had, Marie-Claire accepted her mission without hesitation and indeed traveled through Rwanda and surrounding countries teaching people about that rosary.

When asked to describe the Holy Mother's features, Marie-Claire said that if the world's greatest poet were ordered to describe Mary's beauty with words, he'd throw away his pen and abandon his craft forever. "Her beauty is as great as her love for her children," she explained. "It's beyond human comprehension."

The Virgin had a nickname for Marie-Claire that showed she had a soft spot for the visionary. Mary loved the girl's open nature, childlike naïveté, and great passion for life—a passion so great that Marie-Claire became the only person in recorded history to challenge the Blessed Mother to a fistfight. Whatever the reason, Mary's nickname for Marie-Claire was "the Cherished of the Blessed Mother," and she often favored the seer by granting her requests.

For example, Marie-Claire once asked if her sister, who'd died a year before, was in heaven. The Virgin replied that she was in a place of suffering—she was in purgatory, waiting to be allowed into heaven.

"I know she wasn't perfect and has to spend some time in purgatory to atone for her sins before entering paradise. Yet my family has said so many prayers asking for your intercession to bring her to heaven that my sister should be there by now," the young woman quietly complained.

"Praying for your departed love ones is of great comfort to them and of great help for the souls in purgatory, but people still must work to earn a place in heaven," Mary replied patiently.

In an apparition a few days later, she gave Marie-Claire happy news: "Child, be glad, for today your sister entered heaven and joined your father."

"Thank you!" the girl cried with happiness. She then begged the Holy Mother to show her her dad, who'd died many years before.

"No, child. You will see him when you are in heaven."

Marie-Claire was so saddened that the Blessed Virgin couldn't deny her completely. "I will show you only part of your father, who is waiting to greet you in God's kingdom," Mary said.

"Oh yes, those are my father's feet!" Marie-Claire exclaimed, as tears of happiness streamed down her face. "It's him! He's in paradise!" She then let out a deafening scream that startled the hundreds who'd gathered at the school to witness her apparition. They hadn't heard Our Lady's part of the conversation, which Marie-Claire later reported on. But no one in the audience could mistake Marie-Claire's scream for anything other than what it was: pure joy.

Everyone who witnessed the exchange was profoundly moved by the Virgin Mary's gracious act, along with Marie-Claire's elated cry of recognition, which someone later described as "the sound of a child's love for a parent echoing between Earth and eternity."

SOON AFTER MARIE-CLAIRE'S APPARITIONS BEGAN, the Blessed Mother appeared to each of the visionaries separately and told them that she'd come to them, one after the other, in the courtyard of the school on March 25. She instructed them to gather all 120 students together, and have everyone kneel down during the apparitions and pray the rosary as an act of penance for having persecuted the visionaries. Our Lady said that if the students agreed, she'd grant them all a gift: she promised that every student who attended Kibeho High School for the next six years would complete her education and graduate with a diploma. The promise may sound insignificant to other parts of the world, but in Rwanda such an achievement was completely unknown. Poverty, illness, and the extreme shortage of school placements ensured that only a few students from any one school would complete their education and graduate.

A number of the students scoffed when the visionaries relayed Mary's promise. Yet the guarantee of receiving a full education in one of the world's poorest countries was too great for them to ignore, so most of them showed up at the appointed time. The Protestant and Muslim students, however, refused to do this "Catholic practice"—because they weren't Catholic, they didn't believe that the Virgin Mary cared about them. But Mary had told Anathalie that she didn't look at religion; all people were her children, regardless of their beliefs. She instructed Anathalie to have these Protestants and Muslims pray the rosary not as Catholics, but as her children, and they'd be awarded as all the others.

As Anathalie told the non-Catholic girls, "We're all her daughters, and she loves us all equally. Performing an act of penance is a way of telling God that you're truly sorry for any sins you've committed. The penance Mary is asking for is only to kneel, think about the things you've done that are bad, and honestly tell God you're sorry for doing them.

"Our Lady has never told me that people should convert from their religions, but she loves us so much that she begs us to convert our hearts and love to our Father—that's what she means by 'conversions.' She says that the best way to achieve this is by praying the rosary, which isn't only for Catholics. It's a tool anyone can learn to use to talk to God. But all Mary's asking of you right now is to kneel and say a prayer of forgiveness, using the rosary as children of the mother of God, not as Catholics—in return, you'll get a diploma."

There was much eye-rolling at Anathalie's long-winded explanation, which sounded silly and improbable to these girls. Even so, every student knelt and prayed for forgiveness while the three visionaries communicated with the Blessed Mother. When the apparitions ended, Anathalie was exhausted, but she told the students that Mary wept with joy because they'd all prayed so sincerely, and she wanted to congratulate them in advance for having graduated with honors.

Not all of the students expected the Virgin to fulfill her promise, and the majority probably didn't even believe that she was watching them. But every single girl went on to graduate from Kibeho High School, as did all those who attended the school for the next dozen years until it was shut down during the genocide.

But all that lay ahead in the years to come.

At the time, the school was trying to understand the significance of having another visionary in its midst. To some, it was a third miracle conclusively proving that the Holy Mother was indeed visiting Kibeho; to others it was terrifying evidence that demonic possession was spreading through the student body like a virus.

For the school director, Marie-Claire's conversion was a complete disaster. Since Anathalie had surfaced as a second visionary, scores of Rwandans from across the country were showing up at the school every day demanding to witness an apparition. So many people were milling about that the director told these girls that if they insisted on having apparitions, they had to have them in the courtyard outside, not in the dormitory. Fortunately, Alphonsine and Anathalie announced that the Blessed Mother approved of the move, which would allow more people to hear her messages.

The director now worried that as news of a third visionary spread, thousands of individuals would flock to Kibeho, and her school would be completely overrun. She was right to worry, because that was exactly what was about to happen.

❀ ❀ ❀

Chapter 7

My Father's Pilgrimage

Throughout the spring and early summer of 1982, my father had followed the visionaries' apparitions and messages almost as closely as I had and was now a complete believer. When he finally left for his pilgrimage to Kibeho, the rest of the family stood in the front yard to bid him farewell. Tears ran down my face as he kissed my mother and appointed Aimable, the eldest son, man of the house during his absence.

"Don't look so sad," Dad said to me softly, leaning down and gently brushing a tear from my cheek. "I'm going to say a prayer to the Virgin especially for you."

With that, he slung his canvas bag over his shoulder and walked through our gate toward the road. As he turned to wave good-bye, a chorus of 300 happy voices united in song drifted into the yard as the long procession of Kibeho-bound pilgrims passed by our home. Dad joined the front of the line beside Father Rwagema, who'd organized the journey.

I watched silently as my neighbors set off on a spiritual journey to show their love and devotion to the Blessed Mother. Some were maybe 60 years of age, but they moved quickly, walking four abreast along the rugged dirt road that wound precariously southward over miles of mountains and valleys toward Kibeho. The men and women faced a hard journey of several days and nights, but they were all smiling, knowing that any hardship was well worth the sacrifice. The song they sang praising Mary's Divine love echoed joyously through the hills as they headed down the road and out of sight:

Beautiful mother, we are coming to thank you,
You, who gave us the gift of the holy rosary,
The rosary that explains to us the joy,
The sorrows, and your crowning as
Queen of Heaven and Earth.

Let us come to you, Mary, you are full of joy,
When you conceived Jesus,
When you visited your cousin Elizabeth,
When you gave birth to Jesus,
When you offered him in the temple,
When you saw him in Jerusalem teaching.

Let us come to you, Mary, in your sorrows,
When your child was in agony,
When he was beaten,
When they crowned him with thorns,
When he carried the cross to Calvary,
And when he died on the cross.

Let us come to you, Mary, in the glory you were given,
When Jesus was resurrected,
When the Holy Spirit came over the disciples,
When you were raised into heaven,
When you were made Queen of Heaven and Earth.

Dear brothers and sisters, come to our mother,
Say your rosary from the heart,
Be happy and let's remember our dear mother,
Who loves us beyond measure.

Since my father wouldn't be able to keep in touch with us during his pilgrimage, I prayed morning and night that he'd arrive home safely and report with certainty that the visions of Mary were real. After two weeks, I began sitting in our backyard each afternoon, hoping to be the first to welcome him home. We had a spectacular view of Lake Kivu from our yard, and on the evening my dad returned from Kibeho, I was so entranced by the reflection of the setting sun's shimmering reflection on the water that I didn't hear the pilgrims singing as they approached our house.

Suddenly my father was behind me, and I jumped at the sound of his voice. "It's hard to decide which is prettier: the sunset on the lake or the little girl watching it," he remarked, enveloping me in a huge hug.

As a child I never felt safer or more loved than when my father held me in his arms. Now I wanted to share a private moment with him before my brothers discovered that he'd returned. So, while wrapping my arms tightly around his neck, I asked, "Dad, did you hear her? Could you feel that she was there?"

"Oh yes, sweetheart, she was there. Her love was all around us, and she shone a thousand times more beautifully than the sunset on this lake. There is no way to describe the love one feels in Kibeho. . . . When you see the look on the faces of the visionaries as they listen to Mary, and then you hear the love in their voices while they speak to her, you feel as though you've been given a glimpse of heaven. And I kept my promise: I said a prayer to the Blessed Mother for you. I told her how much you loved her and asked her to look after you for the rest of your life. Now let's go inside, and I'll tell all of you every detail of my wonderful trip," he said, playfully tossing me across his shoulder and carrying me into the house.

MY FATHER WAS LEANER THAN HE'D BEEN WHEN HE LEFT. He was also in better health and higher spirits than he'd been for months—his eyes sparkled, and his smile was full of life. Any trace of doubt or misgiving he'd once had about the Kibeho apparitions had vanished entirely during his pilgrimage; his voice was now reverent and joyful as he spoke about the visionaries. Clearly, whatever he'd witnessed had strengthened his already deep faith in God.

Mom fed Dad his first decent meal in days, and then he sat us all down in the living room and recounted every stage of his journey. "The roads were very bad," he began. "In fact, they were often impassable because of mud slides and fallen rocks. And sometimes we had to hack our way through thick bush and wade across streams and small rivers. We walked 30 miles a day, maybe more. It was exhausting, but no one—not even the eldest among us—complained or suggested that we turn around.

"Most of us had no idea how long the journey was going to take, so we didn't bring enough food with us.

Since many were famished by the end of the first day, we all put our provisions together and marked the beginning of our pilgrimage with a communal feast. After we ate, we prayed to the Holy Mother to watch over us and provide for our needs. That first meal together exhausted our food supply.

"That night we camped in the forest. We built a campfire and had a truly old-fashioned Igitaramo. We sang songs about the Virgin, and Father Rwagema asked us to share stories about how she had touched our lives. When it was my turn, I told them that the greatest gift Mary had given me was a healthy baby girl, whom I named Ilibagiza in her honor—because it means 'shining and beautiful in body and soul,' just like Our Lady—and Immaculée for the Blessed Mother's immaculate heart."

"Oh, Dad," I said quietly, very moved. The trip *had* changed him: he'd never been so open with his emotions, and he'd made me so happy that I felt like crying. My brothers rolled their eyes and asked him to please get back to the story.

"Vicente, a pilgrim who joined us from Father Clement's parish, asked me, 'Isn't naming a girl after the Virgin Mary putting too much pressure on her? How is she going to live up to such a name?'" our father continued. "I said that she doesn't have to live up to it, but what better life could she have by trying to do so? Besides, when I looked at her the first time, I felt Mary with me." He smiled at me, and I felt so much love coming my way.

"Anyway, we had a good Igitaramo," Dad went on, "and we were gathering dried banana leaves to make up our beds when we heard a leopard growling. Many in our group were frightened, since we were all going to be sleeping out in the open with no protection. So some broke tree branches and used bark to lash together about 30 crosses that we planted in a circle around our camp. After that, everyone slept like babies.

"When we got up the next morning, we discovered that someone had visited our campsite during the night and left gifts. Beside one of the wooden crosses sat two huge bags full of rice and beans, which was enough to feed our entire group of 300 for days. We knelt in prayer, thanking Mary for answering our petition to provide for us. We were sure that she was walking with us on our pilgrimage.

"At every village we came upon, people asked if we were Kibeho pilgrims and invited us into their homes. They gave us milk and let us use their facilities to clean ourselves—yes, all 300 of us! Imagine that! People think Mary is blessing Rwanda, and they want to help folks go to her so that she'll stay.

"Whenever one of us stepped on thorns or twisted an ankle, we immediately offered our pain to God and continued walking. Some discomfort and suffering was important on the pilgrimage because it made us reflect upon the Holy Mother's suffering and got us in the spirit to hear her. Besides, if Jesus didn't complain about his suffering, how could we cry over a thorn?

"On the third day, we arrived at a washed-out bridge that spanned a river too deep and swift for us to cross, so we were forced to walk many miles out of our way. We were lost in thick bush, and when the sun set, we didn't know which direction to take the next day. We made camp and prayed for guidance. Two hours later, we saw eight stars in the night sky forming the shape of a cross . . . none of us had ever seen those stars before, and we knew that it was Mary guiding us to Kibeho. In the morning we walked out of the bush in the direction of the cross of stars and made our way to a path that led us to a road just outside of Kibeho."

My father had us completely hypnotized with his story, and he had yet to mention a word about the visionaries. He stretched his arms above his head and let out a great yawn.

"Oh my," he said. "I've had too many nights without proper sleep and wouldn't want to do Our Lady a disservice by repeating the messages I heard at Kibeho while I'm groggy. Let's go to bed, and I'll tell you about it in the morning."

"No!" I protested. "You have to finish your story! Tell us about the visionaries and the apparitions! You can't stop now!"

"Immaculée's right!" my mother and three brothers said in unison.

"Well, if you all insist," Dad replied with a laugh. He then went on with his account: "We saw the crowd of people before we could see the village. There were thousands and thousands of pilgrims from every corner of Rwanda camped along the hills surrounding Kibeho. It was still early morning, and the air was streaked with smoke from cooking fires.

"We found a place to camp not far from the school. A wooden platform had been set up for the visionaries to stand on, and the boards had been carpeted with straw and covered with hundreds of wildflowers that pilgrims had tossed up. By the flowers sat jars of water, and I was told that Mary blessed them during the apparitions so that the visionaries could sprinkle water on the crowd as a blessing.

"Alphonsine was speaking later that afternoon, so we spent the day talking with other pilgrims, singing, and praying our rosaries. There was a tremendous sense of fellowship, nothing like I've experienced in this country before. And I met many people from outside Rwanda as well—some who'd walked for weeks from Tanzania and Uganda.

"Like our group from Mataba, most of the pilgrims didn't bring enough food with them. It turns out that there was nowhere to buy anything to eat in Kibeho, and we had to walk a mile just to fetch drinking water. But I never heard anyone complain about being hungry or thirsty. I saw a lot of very sick people, too, some of whom had been carried there in hopes of a miraculous cure. And many folks had infected sores on their feet because they were too poor to afford shoes and had walked to Kibeho barefoot.

"Yet no one seemed worried. Mary was so close that we just sat down and waited for a miracle."

❀ ❀ ❀

The original three visionaries at Kibeho High School in 1982. From left, Anathalie, Marie-Claire, and Alphonsine.

Pilgrims flock to Kibeho in the early 1980s.

Visionary Anathalie holding rosaries for the Holy Mother to bless during an apparition.

Visionary Alphonsine is recorded during an apparition in 1982.

Visionary Stephanie during an apparition.

Visionary Segatashya during an apparition. Jesus had just told him to drink holy water on the podium to quench his spiritual thirst.

Visionary Marie-Claire during an apparition, receiving her mission from the Blessed Mother to teach the Rosary of the Seven Sorrows to the world. 🌹

Visionary Agnes during an apparition on the podium. 🌹

Visionary Anathalie collapses at the end of an apparition.

The first visionary, Alphonsine, in communication with the Virgin Mary.

Visionary Anathalie on the podium during a 1983 apparition.

Alphonsine being recorded and tested by doctors during an apparition.

Visionary Valentine during a 1992 apparition.

Pilgrims celebrating the Feast of Our Lady of Kibeho on November 28, 2006, the 25th anniversary of the first apparition. The yellow containers they hold are filled with water for the Virgin Mary to bless.

During the 25th anniversary, pilgrims walk in prayer from Kibeho Church, where 5,000 parishioners were killed during the genocide, toward Our Lady's shrine.🌹

Aerial photo of the shrine, taken in 2007.🌹

Our Lady of Kibeho looks out from the shadows toward pilgrims gathered at her shrine in 2007.

In front of the Chapel of the Seven Sorrows. From left, Father Leszek Czelusniak, director of the CANA Center at Kibeho; me; Veneranda, who was honored for saving lives during the genocide; the visionary Anathalie, who still lives in Kibeho; and my friend Tim Van Damm, who was making his first Kibeho pilgrimage.

The CANA Center, run by the Marian Fathers in Rwanda. The 18-foot-tall statue of the Divine Mercy of Jesus is in the middle of the picture. It's located just one mile from Our Lady of Kibeho's shrine.🌹

Me beneath the statue of the Divine Mercy of Jesus, along with some local schoolchildren who often pray at the shrine.🌹

Local women helping to build the expanding shrine at Kibeho.◉

Workers preparing the foundation for a
new building where pilgrims can rest.◉

Lending a hand during the construction to improve Our Lady's shrine.

Our Lady of Kibeho.

Researching this book. Here I interview Dr. Muremyangango Bonaventure of the bishop's Commission of Enquiry, which investigated the apparitions and visionaries. When the commission was formed in 1982, Dr. Bonaventure was the only psychiatrist in Rwanda. 🌐

Gathering information for the book by interviewing Father Muhiligi, who was a theologian on the Commission of Enquiry. 🌐

The Pope's envoy to Rwanda, third from left, blessing pilgrims during the 25th anniversary of Our Lady's arrival in Kibeho. His presence was another major public endorsement by the Vatican of Kibeho's rare status as an approved Marian apparition site.

With Bishop Augustin Misago, who, after 20 years of investigation, approved Kibeho as a Marian apparition site in 2001. To date he has acknowledged the authenticity of the visionaries Alphonsine, Anathalie, and Marie-Claire.

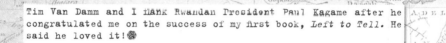

Tim Van Damm and I HANK Rwandan President Paul Kagame after he congratulated me on the success of my first book, *Left to Tell*. He said he loved it! ◉

Pilgrims watching in wonder as the sun spins and miraculous images of the Virgin Mary and the holy cross appear in the sky above Kibeho in 2007. Miraculous visions and cures continually occur there to this day. ◉

My darling children, seven-year-old B.J. and his nine-year-old big sister, Nikki. The kids are smiling after trying on their new Our Lady of Kibeho T-shirts.

Chapter 8

Dad Sees
the Visionaries

The first time my father saw Alphonsine, he was struck by how young she looked and completely taken by her humble demeanor and shy smile. A great cheer went up when she appeared on the platform, and the crowd surged toward her with such force that he thought he may be crushed. But when the girl lifted her rosary, the crowd stopped moving and fell silent. Dad said that for a moment, the only thing you could hear was the rattling of 10,000 rosaries being lifted in unison.

The Blessed Mother had told Alphonsine during her previous apparition that she'd appear that day at 5:15 P.M., which was 20 minutes away. As she waited for the Holy Mother to appear, the young lady led the crowd in prayer.

"As long as I live, I will never forget the moment the Virgin Mary appeared to Alphonsine," my father vowed to my mother, my brothers, and me. "The girl was reciting a Hail Mary when her body suddenly convulsed, as if a jolt of electricity had shot through her, yet the look on her face was one of total love. Her eyes were transfixed, locked on the sky, and brimming with tears of happiness. I knew that she had to be looking at the Virgin—nothing else could have created that expression.

"Alphonsine reminded me of you, Immaculée. She spoke to the mother of God as casually as you speak to your own mother. Her first words to Mary were basically, 'Oh, hi! I'm so happy to see you again. It's been way too long . . . how are you, Mom?' We were put off a bit by her informality, but then we realized that she was just a sweet kid talking to her mother."

My dad compared the two hours Alphonsine spoke that day to being in a room with someone who was talking on the telephone: "We could only hear her side of the conversation, and then we had to wait until Mary finished responding to her before the girl said something else back. At first it was really just small talk, with Alphonsine telling Mary about what she'd been up to since the last time they'd spoken, such as what mark she'd gotten on a recent math test, and she seemed to be answering questions about how her classmates and friends were doing."

Dad shared that Alphonsine spent much of her time dancing and singing beautiful songs that the Holy Mother had taught her. He wanted us to hear one of these songs from heaven, called "Turakwambaza Mubyeyi" ("We Are Calling upon You, Mother"), so he did something we rarely heard him do—he sang:

Queen of Heaven and Earth,
We call upon you, Mother,
Be our advocate to Jesus,
Teach us to love him and to do his will,
Bring him into the world,
So we can help him to save mankind.

Queen of Heaven and Earth,
Mother of God and mother of ours,
Listen to those who call upon you,
Help them to know God better,
Pray for them and intercede for them.

You lived on Earth, Mother,
You know how easily we get lost,
We need to know the true way,
The way that Jesus taught,
Pray for us that he sends us his messengers.

Look at the young people trying to follow Jesus,
Pray for us to have purity of heart,
Pray that we commit to the goods of heaven,
So that we can be his messengers.

They are those who don't understand
Why Jesus wants us to follow him,
Pray for them and pray for us,
That we may know his will and believe his words,
So we can grow to be his true messengers.

My father continued on with what happened after the song. "Father Rwagema had told us that Alphonsine has received many secret messages for government leaders, and that the president has already come to Kibeho with his wife and family at least twice to see her," he explained. "Now as we stood there, she received a message for the bishop, who Father Clement says has talked to Alphonsine at least once. The girl kept nodding at the sky and saying, 'Yes, Mom, I'll make sure that I give him that message exactly as you told me to . . . yes, darling, I understand that I'm only to give the message to the bishop himself.'"

"Wow, Alphonsine really speaks with the president and the bishop?" I asked, in awe of the girl who was only a few years older than I was.

"Apparently she does," Dad said. "Clement told me the bishop wants to ensure that these apparitions are carefully monitored by the Church, so he set up two special commissions to investigate the visionaries and their apparitions. One commission has doctors to see if the girls are sick or mentally ill, while the other commission has priests to make sure the messages don't contradict what's in the Bible or come from the devil . . . can you imagine what could happen if everybody had been listening to the devil all this time?"

My father paused. "The bishop would never have allowed so many folks to gather like that if he had many doubts," he went on, "and Alphonsine's messages didn't sound diabolical. In fact, she insisted that Mary said the world has become too sinful, and she urged us all to pray for people to convert their hearts and love to God. The Holy Mother wants us all to pray for sinners to convert, to treat each other with love, to treat our bodies as temples of the Lord, and not to commit sins of the flesh. Basically, what she said was for us to live a life closer to Jesus. And she told us to pray the rosary every day because every chaplet prayed to Mary is a blessing to her, and she promises to return those blessings many times over."

Years later, I recalled what Dad said about the rosary bringing blessings when, because of the government's ethnic quotas, we didn't think that I'd ever get into a good high school. After I was accepted by the best private high school in Rwanda—and among the best schools in all of Africa—my father told me that Alphonsine's words that day had inspired him. He'd prayed the rosary for years, asking Mary to get me into the best school despite impossible odds.

"Alphonsine led us in many more prayers," Dad stated now. "One of them went: 'Please bring us together as one family in Christ, so we can all be his disciples and together spread his word throughout the globe. Let us have one heart in Christ so that we live as one. And please grant me what I ask for: not money or riches or the pleasures of the world, but that we all may live on this earth together in peace, kindness, and happiness.'"

He told us that Alphonsine loved being with Mary so much that she cried her eyes out when the Virgin said good-bye. To bid her farewell, the young woman sang Our Lady's favorite hymn, "the Magnificat," the same hymn the Virgin herself sang when she was pregnant with Jesus:

My soul proclaims the greatness of the Lord
And my spirit rejoices in God my Savior,
He has looked with favor on His lowly servant.
From this day all generations will call me blessed,
The Almighty has done great things for me
And holy is His name.

He has mercy on those who fear Him,
From generation to generation.
He has shown strength with His arm
And has scattered the proud in their conceit,
Casting down the mighty from their thrones
And lifting up the lowly.
He has filled the hungry with good things
But has sent the rich away empty.
He has come to the aid of His servant Israel,
To remember His promise of mercy,
The promise made to our ancestors,
To Abraham and his children forever.

MY FAMILY WAS JUST STARING AT MY FATHER, trying to take in everything he'd been telling us. But there was so much more he'd seen, so he kept on with his story.

"When she finished singing, Alphonsine fell flat on her face like a sack of stones," Dad said. "We were sure she'd died because she didn't move a muscle. But eventually two nuns lifted her up by her arms and carried her off the platform.

"There was a special ceremony the next day in honor of the Blessed Mother's appearance in Kibeho. There was beautiful music, and hundreds of people danced and sang hymns in front of the podium. Later in the day a large group of girls from the high school was dancing at the front of the crowd in very colorful dresses, when Marie-Claire walked to the podium with her rosary. She'd only begun to pray when she fell into the same rapture that had overcome Alphonsine the day before: her body convulsed, her hands slapped together in front of her in prayer, and her face completely transformed with a similar look of love. Both girls seemed to have departed normal time and space and entered a rapturous dimension beyond our comprehension.

"Oblivious to the celebration and the singing and dancing that surrounded her, Marie-Claire seemed unhappy. She stopped looking up at the sky and instead just stood there, rocking back and forth. Finally, when she did look up, she began apologizing to the Holy Mother for something and seemed genuinely upset. She asked, 'Mother, why do you ignore me? Won't you speak to me? Why do you take so long to answer me?' She sounded so sad and hurt.

"But a few minutes later, the young woman threw her arms out wide, as though she were trying to embrace the entire sky. And then she looked directly down at the girls dancing in front of her and said, 'Thank you . . . oh, thank you, Mother. I see them! I see *you!* It's a wonder to watch you play with your children. We love you so much, Mother!'"

Marie-Claire then began dancing and clapping with her singing classmates. Dad couldn't remember the words to the song, but he said it was about Jesus calling his disciples to follow him to spread the good news that the son of God had arrived.

This part about Marie-Claire dancing with the children surprised us, since the visionaries had always said that they could only see Mary hovering over a field of flowers during their apparitions and that the flowers were the people in the crowd. Yet Father Clement later shed some light on what had happened.

Clement had heard an interview Marie-Claire gave to a priest in which she explained that when she entered her state of ecstasy that day, she was too embarrassed to look at Our Lady because she hadn't done something she'd been asked to do. He remembered her explanation:

> Our Lady called out my name right away, but I was too ashamed and afraid to look at her. She called my name again, but I still wouldn't look at her. Then she asked, "Child, what is the matter? Why do you not look at me when I call you?" I kept my head bowed and said nothing. "Child, tell me why you do not look at your own mother?" she asked again and again.
>
> Finally I confessed to her that I hadn't been true to her and hadn't faithfully fulfilled her request. But the mother of God is so forgiving that right away she said, "Do not be silly, child, that does not matter. Look at me!" But when I glanced up, she wasn't looking at me, so I thought she was disappointed in me. She was looking at the flowers near my feet, but not at me! I called out to her, but she continued to gaze at the flowers.
>
> When I asked her why she was ignoring me, she replied, "My child, I am sorry." Now she was looking right at me and smiling with great kindness. "I was distracted watching all my lovely children who are dancing and singing so beautifully for me. I love when my children play with me so innocently." Then I knew she saw what I couldn't. I said that all I could see were flowers around me whenever she spoke to me, and would she please just this once allow me to see the people who'd come to Kibeho?
>
> "Your prayer is granted, child," she said. I instantly saw my schoolmates dancing and singing in front of me and that the Blessed Mother had joined them. They couldn't see her, but she was indeed standing in the middle of the singing girls, smiling at them warmly and holding her hands out to them, accepting their gift of music and dance. She was very, very happy.

Dad now remarked that the singing and dancing had continued for another half hour before Marie-Claire resumed her private visitation with Our Lady. He told us, "Sometimes Marie-Claire, like the other visionaries, made it possible for us to know what the Virgin was saying by using phrases like, 'So you're saying that you want me to say . . .' or, 'The message you want people to know is that . . .' and then she'd deliver the message."

One conversation Marie-Claire had with the Queen of Heaven was about why she'd chosen to come to Rwanda, a country so poor and tiny that nobody in the world cared about it or even knew it existed. Dad said, "She told the Holy Mother, 'No one believes you would come to such a poor place. What should I tell them? Why *are* you here?'

"Mary explained that she'd come here *because* it's such a little, unknown place. She wanted to show the world that God sees and hears all of His children—rich or poor, white or black, man or woman. As they say, we're all created equal in the eyes of the Lord. She also said that Rwanda was special to her because the people here were humble and had a great faith in and respect for God, and they had an especially warm place in their hearts for Mary. She feels the great love for her here.

"But Marie-Claire also told us that Our Lady didn't appear in Kibeho just to speak to Rwandans. She said the Virgin kept repeating the same message: 'When I address myself to you, I am talking to the whole world. I have not come to Rwanda to speak to only those in the parish of Kibeho. When I speak to one person, I speak to all of God's children everywhere.'"

Dad then switched gears, saying, "The young woman brought us serious messages, too, such as the warning that humans' time on Earth is nearing the end and that many of God's children have fallen into sin. Mary told her that she was here to convert hearts back to Jesus and encourage people to say the rosary because it's the most powerful tool of prayer and conversion we have to fight evil and receive God's love.

"Marie-Claire continually expressed that the Virgin was worried about the salvation of the souls of her children, and she kept repeating the same plea over and over: 'Repent, repent, *repent!*' After many hours, the visionary grew quiet and her apparition seemed to be at an end, but then she said something that showed me how deeply Mary knew Rwanda, and she won the hearts of everyone on that field.

"As hundreds of folks were beginning to leave, the girl began to speak again, and what Mary told her reenergized the entire crowd: 'It is not time to say good-bye yet, my children, for our visit has been too short. It is now time for Igitaramo!' Everyone jumped to their feet in anticipation of at least another hour of song."

As I mentioned earlier, Igitaramo is an extremely important part of Rwandan culture that serves as our most cherished form of communication. For Our Lady to initiate Igitaramo showed that she was truly the entire world's Blessed Mother and could adapt to every custom and culture. When she appeared to the children of Fátima, she didn't ask them to join her in an African ritual—no, she came to them in a way that would allow them to understand who she was and what messages she wanted to bring. Later I'd learn more about how Mary appeared to people in different parts of the world, but at that time I only knew about her appearances at Fátima and Lourdes.

How wise you are, Mother, I thought, *to show us that we're all one family and that wherever you are, we're all your children and you love us all!*

"Before and during the apparition, people had placed rosaries and containers of water on the podium for the Virgin to bless," Dad continued. "Marie-Claire began Igitaramo; then, during the last songs, she picked up a container of blessed water, descended from the podium, and began walking through the crowd, sprinkling water on the 'flowers' as blessings and benedictions. Her eyes never left the sky as she did this.

"When the young lady returned to the platform, she was still looking up at Mary. After the last word of her last hymn had passed her lips, she fell backward like a tree, hitting her head on the boards so hard that the sound echoed across the field. But as with Alphonsine, she wasn't injured—after lying motionless for several minutes, she too was helped from the stage by nuns. Later that evening as we talked about the way the girls fell, a pilgrim from another village told me he'd heard Alphonsine say that when she was in the presence of Mary, the Blessed Mother gave her strength and held her up, but when Mary left her, every ounce of strength she had was gone, and she couldn't even stand up on her own."

MY DAD SPENT TWO MORE DAYS IN KIBEHO to see an apparition of the third visionary, Anathalie. He said that she entered her ecstasy in the same manner as Alphonsine and Marie-Claire had, first arriving at the podium to pray the rosary with the faithful crowd. When Mary arrived, Anathalie's body jerked three times, but then joy washed over her face.

She began singing a song the Virgin had prepared especially for her:

The Blessed Virgin is truly the Virgin,
I will pray for her help all day and all night.
I will pray for her help in sorrow,
I will pray for her help with every breath.

When she finished, Anathalie leapt to her feet and stood ramrod straight, like a soldier snapping to attention before a commanding officer. A curious exchange then followed between the Holy Mother and the seer. My father only heard the one side, of course, but it was apparently a conversation Anathalie and Mary had had on previous occasions.

"When Anathalie jumped up like that, we knew the Virgin had asked if she was standing," Dad told us. "The girl replied, 'Yes, Mother, I am standing up. But I understand that you're asking if we're all standing up to make an effort to break away from the earthly things that prevent us from following you.'

"Then Mary asked, 'Are you washing yourselves?' And Anathalie said, 'Mother, you're asking us if we're confessing our sins to God and asking His forgiveness.'

"Finally, the Holy Mother asked, 'Are you paying attention?' And Anathalie said, "'Mother, you're asking us if we're taking care to see you, if we're making sure that we live as you want us to . . . because you show us so much and give us so many signs, yet we see nothing!'"

Dad learned that during Anathalie's first apparition, Mary had told the visionary she'd suffer much in her life, but her suffering was meant as a way to remind us to pray—in despair we often call on God, but we forget to follow His ways or keep praying when our suffering has ended and we're happy again.

After one of her earliest apparitions, it seems that Anathalie had become completely blind for two weeks, but then her sight was miraculously restored. Because of that she often spoke of human beings' blindness to the peace, love, and salvation God offers us every day. On other occasions she lost the ability to speak and to hear for weeks at a time; both ways were intended for her to atone for the sins of others.

"Anathalie told us that no one enters the kingdom of God without having known suffering, for this is how we learn humility and to see what's truly important. All we have to do is think of the great suffering Mary endured watching her son crucified, or of the suffering Jesus accepted for the forgiveness of all our sins.

"At one point during the apparition, Anathalie cried out joyfully, 'Yes, Mother, I know how much you love your children and want to protect our souls! I know that the suffering you offer us comes from the great love you hold for us in your Immaculate heart! You'll always lead us through the road of suffering that you followed yourself, the true road on which we'll meet you in heaven.'"

My brothers and I looked at each other, unsure if we understood why Mary wanted us to suffer. But our father said that enduring suffering is part of building our faith, and only a strong faith will carry us through this life and into the next.

DESPITE THE AMAZING STORY DAD WAS RELAYING, we were all very tired. And Dad, who'd traveled so far and for so long, was particularly exhausted. "Let's go to bed, and I'll tell you more tomorrow," he said. "But first I'm going to let you know how Anathalie's apparition finished that day.

"First of all—and you're going to love this, Immaculée—she let us know that Our Lady wants a basilica built right in Kibeho."

"A basilica?" I asked, having never heard the word before.

"Yes, it's like a cathedral, only a lot bigger. It will be huge, in fact, like a fort," Dad explained.

"Like the castle of God?" I asked excitedly.

"Yes, that's a pretty good description. Like God's castle . . . I like that," my father smiled and continued on. "Anyway, I couldn't hear everything, but the Virgin said that the basilica was to be called 'the Meeting Place of the Dispersed,' whatever that means.

"Anathalie actually walked off the podium to show exactly how big it was supposed to be. She walked so far away I couldn't even see her anymore! We'd be able to put a thousand houses just like ours in a basilica that size and still have room for a thousand more. All the while, she was saying, 'Oh, Mother, how big this church is! How beautiful you've made it . . . such beautiful statues and flowers . . .' She must have walked and talked for two miles—I can't wait until the bishop gets the building plans for that!" he said with a laugh.

Then Dad told us that at another time, the visionary had described a chapel Our Lady wanted built in Kibeho as well: "It's called 'the Chapel of the Seven Sorrows,' after what Mary suffered in her life after Jesus was born. Now this is to be much, much smaller than the basilica, but the description I heard was so beautiful! It sounds like it would be built from roses and gemstones to be of such beauty . . . I don't know any builders in Rwanda who would want to have the Holy Mother as their architect and contractor." Dad laughed again, and it was wonderful to see him so relaxed and happy.

"Once she'd described the basilica," he continued, "Anathalie began singing every song I've ever heard about the Blessed Virgin. Then, after two hours of praying, singing, and giving messages from Mary, the girl looked at the crowd and said, 'Look how many flowers there are in the field today! Our Lady says she knows that many of you have traveled great distances to be here with her. She knows how much you've suffered to be here, that your bodies are sore and your souls are thirsty. She wants me to water her flowers.'

"And then Anathalie reached down for one of the containers of holy water. We thought that she was going to walk through the crowd and sprinkle people with the water as Marie-Claire had done. But as she bent down she looked out at the field and said, 'Oh, Mother, there are so many of them that I can't water them all. Won't you help me?'

"At that moment, it began to rain on the entire crowd. The surrounding countryside remained dry, but all the pilgrims were washed and cooled by the beautiful shower Our Lady blessed us with. I can't describe how that water felt, especially after an entire day beneath the hot sun, except to say I felt as though I'd been baptized again. My spirit felt renewed, and I was so filled with love that I began singing 'the Magnificat' with all of my heart.

"Afterward Anathalie collapsed like the other visionaries had and was led from the stage by the nuns. When the rain stopped and the sun dried our clothes, we all noticed that the shower had also healed the cuts and sores on our feet and legs. I felt as if I'd been touched by the Holy Mother herself, that I'd just experienced a miracle, which of course I had."

Chapter 9

Joy in the Land, and Mary's Seven Sorrows

My father's story about his first pilgrimage to Kibeho made me hunger to join him on his next one, but it wasn't to be. No matter how much I begged, pleaded, or complained, he never let me accompany him to see the visionaries—although he took my two older brothers with him many times. When the roads improved and he could drive to Kibeho, he even took along my mother, despite her severe asthma.

"It's no place for a child," Mom told me. "The crowds are so huge and get so excited that you could be trampled to death in a stampede." Of course she was also a born worrier who was forever concerned about my health and safety. She'd fret for days when I got the sniffles.

"If it's safe enough for the boys, it must be safe enough for me! And you know the Blessed Virgin will look out for me," I'd inform my father, going back and forth between my parents in an effort to wear them down.

They stood firmly together on the issue, however, and never relented. That act of good parenting was the only time I ever really resented them, God forgive me. But I came to accept that they knew what was best for me and stopped pestering them. Fortunately, Father Rwagema attended the majority of apparitions with his tape recorder and played them back for Mataba's kids at least once a week. I memorized everything I heard, committing every message to heart. In bed at night I'd replay the messages in my head until the voices of Alphonsine, Anathalie, and Marie-Claire were as familiar to me as those of my friends and family.

Still, I envied the many men and women who made the pilgrimage to Kibeho, especially when I saw how deeply the Holy Mother touched their hearts. Neighbors who'd been mean to me in the past began speaking to me sweetly; villagers known to be miserly became generous; braggarts were more humble; and I witnessed good deeds and acts of charity everywhere I went.

Father Clement told me that priests were telling him of similar behavior in villages across Rwanda. When I asked why, he summed it up in one word: *repentance.* "The Virgin keeps asking people to repent and come back to God. But repentance isn't just saying you're sorry to Him for bad things you've done," he clarified. "Repenting starts by really *being* sorry for the hurt you've caused to yourself and others. Being truly sorrowful is painful, but it teaches us to walk away from our harmful habits and deeds toward a better life in Christ. That's known as 'walking the road to salvation,' and it looks like that's the road people follow home after a pilgrimage to Kibeho. When folks pass by you on that road, you'll notice that they're a whole lot nicer these days, Immaculée."

What Father Clement said was true—everyone *did* seem nicer. When my brother Damascene returned from his first pilgrimage, for instance, he immediately joined the Legion of Mary and began visiting the sick and elderly in our region. Aimable was more gracious with his time and spent hours helping me with schoolwork, and our father single-handedly built a small wooden chapel where people could pray the Rosary of the Seven Sorrows.

"The Blessed Mother told Marie-Claire that she wanted everyone to learn and pray with it as often as possible," Dad explained as I watched him hammer the chapel together, board by board, nail by nail. "People will want to say Our Lady's special prayer more often if they have a special place to do it in."

That night a radio program rebroadcast an apparition in which Marie-Claire shared the message my father had been referring to. The young lady repeated what the Blessed Mother had told her word for word:

> What I am asking you to do is to repent. If you say the Rosary of the Seven Sorrows and meditate on it well, you will find all the strength you need to repent of your sins and convert your heart. The world has become deaf and cannot hear the truth of the word. Today people no longer know how to apologize for the wrong they do through sin; they put the son of God on the cross again and again.
>
> That is why I have come here. I have come to remind the world—and especially you here in Rwanda, where I still can find humble souls and people who are not attached to money or wealth—to hear my words

with open hearts. Pray my Seven Sorrows rosary to find repentance.

Wow, I've got to get one of those special rosaries! I thought. I prayed for Mary to send me one, and she did (through my dad) a week later.

Father Clement told me that the seven medals on this rosary represented each of the seven sorrows of Mary. The first sorrow was when a holy man named Simeon told Mary that her newborn son would change the world but suffer greatly, and that her son's suffering would pain her like a sword stuck into her heart. The second sorrow was the dangerous flight Mary, Joseph, and Jesus made to live as exiles in Egypt when Jesus was being hunted by King Herod's death squads. The third sorrow was when 12-year-old Jesus was lost in Jerusalem for three days. The fourth sorrow was when Mary witnessed her son's agony on his way to Calvary. The fifth sorrow was watching Jesus suffer on the cross. The sixth sorrow was receiving her son's body as it was lowered from the cross. Finally, Mary's seventh sorrow was placing her beloved boy in a tomb.

The Rosary of the Seven Sorrows, I discovered, had been used by Christians for hundreds of years, but had somehow become lost in history. Until, that is, after Marie-Claire's apparition—at which point the special rosaries began to appear all over Rwanda.

As far away as I was from Kibeho, when I prayed with my Rosary of the Seven Sorrows, meditating deeply on the story associated with each medal, I felt the Holy Mother kneeling beside me. The love she felt for her son, as well as her suffering as a mother, overwhelmed me. The magnitude of her sacrifice was beyond my comprehension and made all my childish concerns and complaints seem petty in comparison. But the strength of her love, which I could see reflected in each tale, is what truly moved me.

Mary knew who her son was, and from his earliest days was aware of the pain that awaited him (and her). Yet through all those years, she supported him with the love of a mother, standing by him while he was whipped, beaten, and crucified. And she was there for him when he drew his last breath. I realized that Our Lady, whose soft and gentle voice enthralled the visionaries, had rock-solid strength. It was the rock upon which I would build my faith in God, the strength that would sustain me through whatever sorrows life held in store for me.

THE CHAPEL MY DAD BUILT WAS OPEN TO people of all religions, and the doors were never locked. Mary's message about learning to pray her special rosary was the one he most took to heart. Thus, the last nail he hammered into the wall of the chapel was used to tack up a list of instructions on how to pray the rosary as the Blessed Virgin had taught Marie-Claire. He spent a great deal of time at the chapel himself, and not just praying the Rosary of the Seven Sorrows—because most people in the village couldn't read, he'd have to explain the instructions he posted.

Pilgrims from northern Rwanda passed through Mataba every day, and Dad made sure that we were as hospitable to them as the kind strangers he'd encountered walking to Kibeho had been. It seemed the entire country was on the move; everyone was in a hurry to get to Kibeho because no one knew when the visions might end. But while people from all walks of life were rushing to hear the words of the mother of God, the leaders of the Catholic Church had remained out of sight and almost silent about the events in that village.

I came to learn that the Church does not hasten to embrace modern miracles. Declaring a miracle to be true, such as the apparitions of the Blessed Mother, was risky business for it. If the Vatican approved an apparition that later turned out to be a hoax or the ravings of a lunatic, the Church would be humiliated—and the credibility of centuries of Church dogma and doctrine could be called into question. The Vatican avoids such risks and urges its clergy and parishioners to be extremely cautious about accepting an alleged supernatural event as true.

The Vatican has a long list of criteria an apparition must meet before it's even eligible for the consideration of top ecclesiastical officials. Those claiming to have visions, such as the young people in Kibeho, are subject to a battery of physical and psychological tests to expose their motivations and determine their sanity. Their personal lives, history, habits, friends, and family are all thoroughly investigated to assess the supposed visionaries' moral character and depth of faith. It can be an excruciating experience, with no guarantee of a quick outcome. The Church might immediately dismiss an apparition as fraudulent, delusional, or the work of the devil. Or it might spend decades deliberating whether an apparition is likely to be true, false, or should remain indeterminate.

Even when the Vatican does take the rare step of approving an apparition, such as with Fátima and Lourdes, the approval is not necessarily a declaration of truth. The Vatican may tacitly *endorse* an apparition site, which Pope John Paul II did in 1991 when he prayed at the shrine of the Virgin of Fátima. But the Catholic Church never issues edicts or decrees *compelling* its members to believe in any Divine revelation that has occurred since the close of the apostolic age (which ended with the death of the apostle John, author of the book of Revelation).

Because the Vatican appears to have wisely adopted a wait-and-see attitude toward modern apparitions, it wouldn't have been inclined to send in a team of experts from Rome to investigate an African schoolgirl who insisted that the Virgin Mary floated down from heaven on a cloud and started chatting with her. Claims of apparitions and miracles tend to be left to the leaders of the local clergy to look into and worry about, and that often takes a great deal of time.

But in Kibeho, Our Lady seemed in a great hurry to be recognized.

Word of the Blessed Mother's appearances moved across Rwanda with the speed and power of a lightning storm, electrifying the faith of countless thousands of Christians, reenergizing the clergy, and transforming Kibeho from a backwater to the most talked-about village in the country. Every attempt by the high school's director and the local priest to keep a lid on the visionaries' far-fetched stories failed completely. In a savagely poor and predominantly Catholic country like Rwanda, people were more than open to receive some good news from heaven, so a miracle was bound to make headlines.

THE ONCE-UNKNOWN NAME OF KIBEHO started circulating by word of mouth and quickly found its way on the radio, the one source of mass communication in the country.

Soon daily broadcasts were keeping even the most remote regions of the country up to date on the latest apparition, and commentators interpreted and debated the Holy Virgin's messages over the airwaves. Newspapers also ran feature stories on the seers as news of the Kibeho miracle spread across the African continent. By the late spring of 1982, Alphonsine, Anathalie, and Marie-Claire were household names and practically celebrities.

What started as a trickle of pilgrims to Kibeho threatened to become a deluge as interest in Our Lady's messages continued to grow. The community didn't have the resources to care for its own impoverished people, let alone a multitude of unexpected and hungry guests. The local residents fed their families with what little food they pulled from the soil around their huts. There weren't any motels or hostels to be found within 100 miles in any direction—and there wasn't a grocery store, a restaurant, or even a single public restroom in town. How could there be? There was no running water or electricity. There wasn't even a road capable of handling any means of transportation larger than a donkey. Kibeho was one of the poorest villages in one of the world's poorest countries.

Now, while the little town had weathered difficult times before, the appearance of the Virgin Mary had sparked a spiritual revolution throughout the entire country, and Kibeho was the rallying point of the faithful.

The local officials weren't equipped for what was about to happen, since neither the regional nor national government had an established protocol for regulating Divine visitations. The area's bishop had planned to observe the visionaries from a distance because he didn't want people to think that he was endorsing the apparitions by attending a visitation prematurely. But after Marie-Claire's emergence as a third seer, he had to take decisive action.

Bishop Jean-Baptiste Gahamanyi assembled a medical commission to examine the visionaries, and then he appointed a theological commission a few months later; together, they were known generally as "the Commission of Enquiry." By the end of 1982—without passing judgment one way or the other on the validity of the apparitions—Bishop Gahamanyi authorized Kibeho as a site for public devotion. A larger podium was built, a fence was erected to safeguard the visionaries and allow journalists easy access, and a modern loudspeaker system was installed so that the growing multitude of pilgrims could hear the visionaries' every word.

And it wasn't a moment too soon—not only had the Blessed Mother selected a new group of visionaries to which she would appear, but Jesus Christ himself was about to arrive in Rwanda.

Chapter 10

Jesus's Odd Choice of Visionaries

Segatashya was the happy, good-looking 15-year-old son of poor peasant farmers from Muhora, one of the most isolated areas in Rwanda (and located not far from the neighboring country of Burundi). He hadn't gone to elementary school, and he was content to work long days in his parents' fields—in fact, he had no ambition in life other than to tend to the land and spend evenings with his parents in their hut.

The boy seemed an especially bizarre choice for a Christian visionary because, like his parents, he was a pagan. Segatashya's mother and father had never been baptized (nor had he), the nearest parish was more than a two-hour walk from his home, and he'd never even set foot in a church. He and his family were illiterate, didn't own a radio, and knew nothing about religion. The boy didn't have the slightest idea who Jesus or Mary were . . . until the afternoon of July 2, 1982.

After a hot morning spent working in the bean field, the young man had just ducked under the shade of a tree to rest.

That's when he first heard the voice of the Lord.

Segatashya explained what happened next during one of the many conversations we had while he was living in the town of Butare, where I was attending university. Segatashya had a job in the school library, and after I learned that a Kibeho visionary was working on campus, I stopped by and visited him as often as possible.

When we first met, I was taken by his friendly smile and kind eyes. I also noted that his voice was much deeper than when I'd listened to his apparitions a dozen years earlier on Father Rwagema's tape recorder. Sometimes the two of us would sit for hours in the library chatting about God. And while he was a very easygoing young man, he was deadly serious about the messages he received from Jesus.

During our initial meeting, Segatashya told me about the day the Lord first spoke to him: "I'd just sat down when I heard a man calling out to me. I thought I was alone in the fields and hadn't seen anyone all morning. So at first I thought the voice I'd heard was just the wind. But then it came again.

"'*You*, my child,' it said, softly and kindly. I didn't feel threatened in any way, but rather experienced a great sense of peace and happiness. When I looked around to see who was speaking, there was no one there.

"'My child,' the man called to me once more; but again, I couldn't see anyone near me.

"'My child,' the voice said a third time. Even though no one was there, I answered, asking the man what he wanted of me.

"'If I give you a message, will you deliver it for me?'

"'Yes, I will,' I replied without hesitation, somehow knowing I couldn't refuse. 'But what's your name, sir? Who shall I say has sent me with a message?'

"'I am Jesus Christ,' he said. 'But when you tell them you come in my name, they may not trust or believe you. For you to prove to me you are capable of being my messenger, go now to the people working in the fields nearby and tell them that Jesus Christ sent you here today to instruct them all to purify their hearts because the day of his return is coming soon. Since they cannot say that they have not been warned, they can prepare themselves.'"

My new friend did as Jesus bid him and went to the nearest field, which belonged to a man by the name of Ngenzi Hubert. Many men stood in front of his house, beating dry beans to extract grain.

Segatashya repeated the message Jesus had given him word for word, only to have the men laugh at him. Although the boy didn't realize it himself, he was standing in front of them stark naked.

"Who did you say sent you?" one of the men asked.

"Jesus sent me with a message that you must cleanse your hearts."

The men fell upon Segatashya and beat him for being blasphemous.

A woman in the yard told him, "Child, look at yourself —you're naked! Do you think anyone will listen to you in that condition when you say that you've been sent by Jesus?"

Just then, he heard Jesus say, "I have made you naked; ask them did not their Lord come into this world naked, and was he not stripped naked before he returned to the kingdom of God? He is the one who has made this miracle happen."

The boy repeated the Savior's words to the men, but this time he walked away before they could beat him again.

"Thank you, my child," Jesus said. "That is enough for today; now turn your face to heaven and look at the one who is talking to you."

"I looked up, and heaven opened," Segatashya told me. "I saw a handsome, dark-skinned man around 30 years old dressed in a long tunic that any Rwandan man might wear."

Jesus told the boy to go to Kibeho, where he was to deliver his messages to many people. When Segatashya arrived, he joined the other visionaries and had many apparitions of the Lord while on the podium. His messages were often about the return of Christ at the "end of days," and he urged all who would listen to repent and purify their hearts. "On Judgment Day, the Lord will show everyone their entire lives," he'd say, "and people will know that they're the authors of their own fate. God will show them their lifetime of deeds, and then that person will go where they deserve to go. Don't think that God doesn't see your sins—the Lord sees every action and knows every thought. Repent, for there is not much time left.

"God doesn't abandon any of His children; He is always waiting for you to say yes to Him and let Him into your hearts. God will never deny you mercy if you have a true conversion in your heart. Jesus is telling me to express to you that life on Earth lasts only a moment, but life in heaven is eternal. So you must pray! No one will reach heaven by good deeds alone, by giving special gifts, or by making compromises. The only way into heaven is through prayers that come from the heart."

The son of God himself taught Segatashya the Lord's Prayer and the origin and meaning of many biblical stories, which he then committed to memory. Many members of the bishop's Commission of Enquiry were amazed by the depth and breadth of the illiterate peasant boy's knowledge of the Bible and theology, as well as by his eloquence in conveying that knowledge.

The young man used those gifts when Jesus sent him on missions to other African nations to deliver the Lord's messages. Miraculously, wherever Segatashya traveled, he was able to learn the local language within a matter of days, sometimes hours. He'd be greeted by huge crowds in each village . . . yet he'd often be persecuted by local authorities who felt threatened by his growing popularity and strange, prophetic messages.

Jesus sent the visionary many spiritual trials and physical dangers as he traveled through the wilderness, and he was often attacked by bandits and wild animals— tests, he said, that Christ sent to strengthen his faith.

When Segatashya was baptized in the Catholic faith, the Savior told him to take Emanuel as his Christian name, which means "God is with us."

ANOTHER MESSENGER WHOM GOD CHOSE to reflect His love for all His diverse children was Vestine Salima, who was born into a Muslim family just ten miles from Kibeho in 1960. Vestine's mother, Charitas Mukangwije, had been raised Catholic but converted to Islam when she married

Vestine's father, Habib Mutangana. Vestine's parents could afford a basic education for her and enrolled her in the elementary school nearest to their home, which happened to be a Catholic school.

While her parents were observant Muslims, Vestine didn't have much interest in either the Islam practiced at home or the Christian religion she studied at school. Still, she believed strongly in a greater power and an afterlife, and she instinctively avoided activities that she sensed were unhealthy for the soul. Unfortunately, attending high school was too expensive for her family, so Vestine's formal education ended after the sixth grade, and she went to work in the fields to help support her parents and siblings.

Vestine had been a serious child, and she grew up to be a serious young woman. She didn't care about new clothes, attending dances, going to parties, or wasting time with idle gossip. She valued family and friends above all and believed money to be the root of all evil. She strove to live modestly, and her greatest desire was to be free of material things. She possessed a kindness people found attractive and was quite pretty, but she was uninterested in courtship or romance and made a deliberate choice to remain unmarried.

The details of her first apparition, which occurred in 1980 while she was tilling soil, are a bit sketchy, since it wasn't reported or officially recorded and lasted only a few minutes. Yet Vestine remembered every detail of what happened. "I was working in the fields when I saw a strange-looking man approaching me, carrying a large stack of books," she later said. "He seemed to come out of nowhere, and with the sun in my eyes, I couldn't see his face.

"'You will preach to many people who will come from far and wide to hear your words,' he told me.

"'Who are you, sir, pursuing me in a bean field with a bundle of books?'

"'I am Jesus, the son of God,' the man replied, and then vanished."

The man never returned to the field, so the young lady wrote the incident off as a mild case of heatstroke. But she often heard the man's voice in her dreams (even when she was awake), recalling each time what he'd told her in the bean field and who he claimed to be. The memory always tugged at her heart, but she put it out of her head and carried on with life. The vision she received two years later, however, could not be brushed aside as easily.

During the night of April 13, 1982, Vestine claims to have been awakened from a deep sleep by a voice telling her it was time to pray. She sat up in bed to find a rosary in her right hand and a group of children sitting in front of her, so she knelt and prayed with the youngsters. When she completed the rosary, she looked up and saw a very sad-looking young woman sitting in a chair.

For some reason Vestine accepted the situation, not questioning the inexplicable appearance of either the woman or the children. It was the lady's deep emotional suffering that concerned her, so she kindly asked, "What makes you so sad, miss?"

"Leave me alone, my child, for my words will hurt you. My pain is great because so many of my earthly children refuse to hear the messages I bring them," the woman replied.

Vestine looked at the rosary in her hand and wondered if it was her prayers that had brought the sad lady to her room. "Miss, I'm not a person who prays much, and never with much passion," she admitted. "I seldom recite the rosary, so what's happening to me? Why are you here?"

The woman looked at Vestine forlornly, but a different voice responded to her question: "Continue to pray," it said.

Vestine recognized the voice immediately. "It's you!" she cried. "You're the one who follows me in my mind!"

"I am your Lord, through the day and through the night. What you have seen, I have shown you; what you have heard has been said by me. It is time to leave your earthly things and the life you know. You must prepare for the mission I shall give you."

Later the Holy Mother appeared to Vestine again, but this time she wasn't a sad woman sitting in a corner—she was as beautiful and full of love as all the other visionaries had described her. In a sweet and soothing voice, she told Vestine that she was "the Immaculate Conception."

"My daughter," Our Lady revealed, "you are being sent on a mission of love. You will remind the world of my son's great mercy and the boundless love he has for his children. Tell them that he offers their souls peace and their hearts happiness beyond imagination. Plead with them to pray to their heavenly mother, for I will give them the strength they need to open their hearts to Jesus and let his love wash away their sins and despair. Tell them to accept his love and they will receive eternal joy. Now go, my child, and preach the loving word of the Lord." Mary then filled Vestine's heart and mind with the many messages she was to carry throughout the land.

Vestine accepted the mission without question—it was a journey she'd make on foot, leading her across the width and breadth of the country and beyond its borders into Zaire, Burundi, Uganda, and Tanzania. This was an exceptionally dangerous expedition for a young woman to undertake alone in Africa, but the Blessed Virgin promised to protect her with love in every town and village she entered, and to comfort her in the darkness of every forest and jungle through which she passed.

Our Lady told Vestine to always carry a tree branch in hand as a walking stick, explaining, "It will be your staff; it will show those you meet that you are on a mission from God, that you are a shepherd of the Lord sent to lead his flock from danger and show them the path."

Mary gave the girl further instructions: "My child, pray your rosary while you walk. When you meet an orphan, treat him as your own child, and give comfort to the troubled and care for the sick. Never refuse any who ask you for help; if your pockets are empty, give them hope. Your every action must be born of kindness, your every word spoken with love. Live as God would have you live, and others will be inspired to do the same.

"By walking the world as a shepherd, you will show my earthly children that the walk to heaven is along a narrow road that is not easy to travel. But the road leading to Satan is wide and easy to follow, because the devil puts no obstacles on the road to darkness."

Vestine said good-bye to her parents and siblings, who'd accepted her vision and Divine calling, and set off from home without fanfare. After receiving her first public apparition at Kibeho in front of thousands, word of her mission quickly spread—her reputation as a visionary and preacher preceded her wherever she went.

I WAS IN MY EARLY TEENS WHEN VESTINE arrived in Mataba, and I'd never seen my village in such a state of excitement and commotion before.

Father Rwagema had been closely monitoring the visionary's travels, and when he discovered that she was in our region, he arranged for her to come to Mataba to preach. He assembled a welcoming committee of at least 500 people; of course given the huge importance placed on hospitality in Rwanda, where "the guest is king," we couldn't just meet her at the edge of town. Rather, all 500 official greeters marched for ten miles to the nearest crossroads to formally invite Vestine and escort her to our village.

My friend Jeanette and I ran along with the eager crowd, ducking between the grown-ups to get to the front of the line. I think I was the first to actually see her emerge into view over a rise in the road, and I noted that she didn't have any bags. However, she moved toward us in short, quick strides, her staff in her right hand.

A great cheer went up when the villagers spotted her, and Father Rwagema thanked her for accepting our invitation to preach. Several men had carried a tall statue of the Virgin Mary to the meeting place and now placed it on a wooden platform, which they lifted to their shoulders as though carrying a stretcher. The statue of the Blessed Mother rose above their heads, and they set off back to town with the rest of us forming a happy procession and Vestine leading the way.

Someone began singing a song that Our Lady had taught Vestine. Soon a chorus of 500 joyful voices joined in, and the words praising Mary's love for her children echoed across the land:

Mother of mankind, you have remained faithful,
Mother of mankind, you have never rested,
You have loved us, in giving us your child
Who wanted to die for us.
Save the sinners, that they too may serve you,
Give sight to the blind
So that they may see what you show them,
Unblock their ears, so that they
May hear what you tell them,
Heal the crippled so that they may stand.

More than 5,000 people turned out to hear Vestine preach. Because no church in the area was large enough to accommodate such a crowd, Father Rwagema led everyone to the center of a bean field so that we could all hear the visionary. Like dozens of other kids, Jeanette and I climbed a tree and sat among the branches as Vestine spoke.

The visionary was very serious and didn't smile at all while she delivered her messages, which often came in short bursts of easily remembered sentences. She also used her staff to draw a large circle in the soil, saying that it represented the world, which was filled completely with the love of the Blessed Mother.

We all watched in fascination as she imparted Mary's wisdom. "The Holy Mother says that her love for you, her children, is greater than the love any earthly mother has ever felt for a child," Vestine reminded us. "Her arms are wide open to embrace all who come to her; she will press you tightly to her bosom and cherish and protect you.

"Our Lady says that she will console you; she hears the prayers of all who call on her, and she watches over you all. She begs you not to follow the road that Satan has built to lead the world away from her son. She says that Jesus is looking for a place to live and begs you with her tears to offer him a home in your heart.

"She states that there are many lights in the world to follow, but there is only one true light—that of God. She's desperate for you to have the wisdom to believe what she tells you and follow His light to the truth; it will give you life. Live with your faith throughout your life. Don't wear it like a coat that you put on and take off, since this won't save you when you die.

"She says, 'Love my son, love each other, and care for the poor and sick. Do not let jealousy and anger into your hearts; fill them with kindness and be willing to forgive. If you are weak in spirit or lacking in faith, pray to me, and I will bring you comfort and strength.'"

Vestine spoke for most of the day, and the people in my village talked about it for years to come. Before she left, I even got to shake her hand. She was the first visionary I ever met, and at the time I thought she'd probably be the last. I've thanked the Blessed Mother many times that this has not been the case.

Chapter 11

Three More Visionaries

One of the most popular visionaries to arrive in Kibeho was 21-year-old Agnes Kamagaju, a shy but happy girl who grew up in a devoutly Catholic home with two sisters and three brothers. Like most Rwandan families, Agnes's struggled for survival, so she left elementary school after the sixth grade to help support the clan. Despite tough economic challenges, the girl always remained cheerful and optimistic. In fact, when I met her in the early 1990s, I found her an absolute joy to be around—she was direct, honest, sincere, and wonderfully empathetic.

Agnes told me that she was lying in bed trying to sleep when Mary first appeared to her on the evening of August 4, 1982. "My eyes were closed, and I was thinking about the many chores waiting for me in the morning when, for no reason, I started feeling very happy," she said. "My happiness was so intense that I started giggling with pleasure, but soon I was laughing so loudly that I woke up my parents, who came to my room to see what was wrong.

"'Nothing's wrong; I'm just really, really happy,' I told them, still laughing. It was the strangest feeling—I guess I was literally overjoyed. My room filled with light, and I saw her standing in front of me. She was beautiful and young, younger than I was . . . just a teenager really, but her eyes were filled with the love that only a mother can possess. She wore a white dress with a blue veil, and the light surrounding her glowed like a crown about her head.

"'God sent me to you with a message,' she said.

"Looking back on it, Immaculée, I suppose I should have been terrified, but I felt safer and more loved than I ever had before. I started laughing even more loudly, and the woman smiled at me and told me to pray the rosary. When I began to do so, I was suddenly out of my room and kneeling beside her in a field of flowers. She pointed to the sky, and I saw a crystal ship floating in the stars. I thought she was showing me the way to heaven.

"'Who are you?' I asked in amazement. She said that she'd tell me her name when she came to see me again. She instructed me to go to Mass the next day and pray, and then she was gone and I was back in my bed, laughing happily again. My parents hollered from the other room, asking again if anything was wrong and why I was so happy.

"'Absolutely nothing's wrong,' I assured them. 'I'm so happy because a woman came to my room and said she had a message for me from God.'

"'Well, if the message *is* from God, you have nothing to worry about,' they retorted. 'Now will you please stop laughing so loudly? We're trying to sleep.'

"Two nights later my room again filled with light, and she was back. She told me she was the Mother from Heaven, and I knew right away that she was the Blessed Virgin. This time, instead of pointing up to the beautiful ship, she pointed down, where a dark pool was spreading across the ground like an enormous puddle of black ink. I was afraid of being sucked into the puddle and drowning in the darkness.

"'That is where people dwell who remain enveloped in the death of sin,' Our Lady told me. 'My son has a mission for you: you are to lead the young people away from the darkness of sin and back into his light.'"

About six weeks later, Jesus himself appeared to Agnes. She told me that he approached her from the distance across a muddy field on a dark day of driving wind and pounding rain. On his back he carried the heavy wooden cross upon which he was crucified. The sky rumbled with thunder, and Agnes trembled as the Lord drew near. "I was so frightened by what I was witnessing that I thought I wouldn't be able to speak. But as he passed me I found the courage to address him," she said.

"'Why do you still carry that with you?' I asked him. He then lifted the enormous cross in front of him and spun it around many times so that I'd see every inch of it from every possible angle. As I watched it spin, my heart was banging against my chest.

"'This is the cross of Christ,' he replied. 'This is the cross that will make both the good and the wicked tremble.'

"I tried to calm myself, but all I could think of to settle my nerves was to sing. So I sang to Jesus, 'The day you will choose those who have followed your will, God, please have mercy on us . . . ' But I was so frightened that I passed out before the second verse. I don't even remember how that first apparition of Jesus ended, Immaculée."

I recall listening to tapes of Agnes's apparitions when I was young and being entranced by the stories my parents and neighbors shared about watching her apparitions, which were always highlighted with phenomenal miracles. It was these extraordinary events, such as the sun spinning in circles or the images of Jesus in the sky, that made Agnes hugely popular with the tens of thousands of pilgrims who flocked to her apparitions.

Now she told me that Jesus returned to her and said her mission was to bring the youth of the world back from sin, especially from sin of the flesh. It was a message I'd heard on tape years before I met her. This is what the Lord said:

> Young people must stop treating their bodies as playthings and instruments of pleasure. So many of the youth are using any means they can to find love and to be loved by others—they have forgotten that true love comes only from God and God alone. Instead of serving Him, they live at the service of money. Young women must make their bodies instruments that will glorify Him, not serve as objects of pleasure for the lust of men. Young men must seek to satisfy the hunger of their spirit, not feed the desires of their flesh. Tell them all to pray to my mother to intercede on their behalf. Tell the youth not to ruin their lives; the wrong way of living can weigh heavily on their future.

Jesus's messages to Agnes for the youth of the world may have seemed prudish and old-fashioned to some. But as I reflected upon her words over the years, I can't help but marvel that they were spoken 25 years ago, just as HIV was silently brewing in dark places and laying waste to thousands of young lives through the epidemic that devastated my country and claimed so many lives around the world.

STEPHANIE MUKAMURENZI WAS JUST 14 YEARS OLD when Our Lady first appeared to her in church, and she's the youngest and the least known of the visionaries. The files the Commission of Enquiry compiled during their investigations of the visionaries report Stephanie as one of seven children and that her father died when she was only ten years old. She was in grade school when her visions started and, like the first three seers at Kibeho High School, she was mercilessly teased and taunted by her schoolmates.

After her first visitation from the Blessed Virgin in May 1982, Stephanie received 14 more apparitions, each with a very similar message: Mary asked her to urge people to let their hearts be converted, to pray honestly, and to love God above all other things.

In one of Stephanie's apparitions that Father Rwagema played for us on his tape recorder in late 1982, the young girl warned people that the devil was busy on Earth laying snares to capture souls to prevent them from reaching God's light: "Our Lady is telling me to say, 'God loves you all, and only God's love is true and everlasting. Satan wants to destroy your souls. You must do everything in your power to resist the temptations he places in front of you, for they will only bring you to darkness.'"

VALENTINE NYIRAMUKIZA HAS HAD the most frequent visitations of any of the visionaries, and she continues to have them to this day.

Valentine was born on February 18, 1965, in the village of Mubuga, far from Kibeho. Like many of the other young seers, she wasn't a particularly religious person, but she did have a strong Catholic faith, attend Mass with her parents each Sunday, and enjoy singing in the church choir. Her first apparition was on May 12, 1982, when she heard a friendly woman's voice calling to her in church: "You there . . . little child."

Valentine looked around the church, but everyone around her had their heads down in prayer. The voice came a second time: "Long life to you, child!" Valentine spun around again; but still, all heads were bowed.

"Where are you?" the voice asked.

"I'm in church," Valentine answered in a whisper.

"What are you doing?"

"I'm listening to the word of God."

"Do you know who is talking to you?"

"No, who are you?"

"I am the mother of God."

That was the extent of the conversation, and Valentine thought that she'd imagined the episode . . . until the Blessed Virgin appeared before her a few days later at home. Valentine's description of Our Lady matches that of the other visionaries: a woman of unparalleled beauty and unimaginable love.

The Queen of Heaven told the girl to join the others in Kibeho and gave her a mission similar to the one she'd given Anathalie: she was to seek penance and willingly and joyfully suffer for the sins of others without complaint. The Holy Mother asked Valentine to pray the rosary every day—and the Rosary of the Seven Sorrows twice a day—for the rest of her life.

Prayer was a central part of Valentine's mission, and I remember listening on the radio to a lesson Our Lady asked her to teach the pilgrims of Kibeho. The young lady had apparently been saying a prayer on the podium when the Virgin asked her to teach all her earthly children how to pray properly. Here's what Mary said all those years ago:

> My children, there are many who want to pray, who try to pray, but do not know how to pray. You must ask for the strength and knowledge to understand what is expected of you. My love goes out to you all, for there are many here who want to reach the road to heaven, but do not have the strength or knowledge to ask for God's help. My dear children, listen to my words, for I will teach you how to pray from the bottom of your hearts.
>
> You must begin your prayers by offering God all you conceal in your soul. God sees your every action and knows your every thought; you can hide nothing from Him. But you must tell Him yourself—you must be willing and strong enough to confess all of your transgressions of body, mind, and spirit to Him. Hold back nothing; admit all your bad deeds and thoughts. Then you must ask for God's forgiveness from the bottom of your heart. Rest assured that if you confess and seek forgiveness sincerely, He will forgive you. By beginning this way, the sins you carried will not distract you from praying sincerely. You can then speak to Him knowing that your heart is clean and your conscience is clear. Pray to Him fervently, make a petition, beg His favor, ask for His blessing; God sees into your soul and knows you seek His help with a repentant heart.

Then, my children, you too must offer forgiveness by asking God to forgive all those who have trespassed against you, all who have caused you suffering or given you insult or injury. Forgive them in prayer and ask God to bless and help them.

Then pray for the spiritual and physical welfare of your relatives, for all of your brothers and sisters, that God may bless them. Then give thanks to Him for having received and answered your prayers. Most important, you must ask God for the strength you need to do His will; ask for the strength not to stray from His light. Pray for the courage and wisdom to walk only the road leading to heaven.

And never forget, my children, to pray for the strength to be humble. Your prayers have no meaning if they do not come from the depths of your heart, and you cannot open your heart to the Lord without humility. I love you, my children. When you lack the strength to pray, ask for my help. Pray for my intercession, and I will strengthen you and bring you to my son and to the Father through your prayer.

Of all the visionaries I've met, Valentine is the one I'd come to know best; in fact, she'd give me a blessing that I've cherished each day of my life. It grieves me that her messages from Mary would one day be twisted and used by evil men to do great harm . . . but that's a part of the story I'll get to later in the book.

THE EIGHT VISIONARIES I'VE TOLD YOU ABOUT—the original three and the five that soon followed—are the best known, most studied, and most highly regarded in Rwanda. They were all specifically told by Mary or Jesus to go to Kibeho to be heard.

We may never know for certain how many other people the mother and son of God appeared to in my country. After these seven young ladies and one young man began sharing their apparitions in front of Kibeho High School, dozens of self-proclaimed visionaries surfaced in every corner of Rwanda claiming to have been visited by the Holy Mother. One member of the bishop's Commission of Enquiry reported at least 140 alleged seers. When asked why they weren't all studied, a member of the theological commission said that there were "just too many rabbits for us to chase."

Many so-called visionaries were quickly dismissed as liars or as suffering from mental illness. But dozens of others were never interviewed or investigated, and their messages—true or false—were never documented. Often these individuals lived in the most remote and inaccessible parts of the country and couldn't easily be found. But even if they had been available for questioning, there simply weren't enough resources to examine so many cases. At the time, Rwanda had one doctor for every 10,000 patients, and only one psychiatrist in the entire country. So the Commission of Enquiry chose, probably wisely, to focus on the visionaries who seemed most credible, appeared the earliest, and were closest to Kibeho. Even that number will vary depending upon whom you ask.

I believe that Alphonsine, Anathalie, and Marie-Claire—whom the Church endorsed—received apparitions from the Blessed Mother. But I also believe what thousands of other Rwandans and many members of the commission do: that Segatashya, Vestine, Agnes, Stephanie, and Valentine were also visited by the Virgin Mary, Jesus, or both; and that they too brought us heaven-sent messages that God wants the world to hear.

Chapter 12

Miracles in the Sky

I never got to Kibeho as a child, but Kibeho always managed to find me.

Some of the most colorful stories about the visionaries reached me as I lay in bed at night, eavesdropping on my parents' late-night conversations with the neighbors outside my window.

One night the conversation turned to miracles. My mind jumped back several weeks, recalling the afternoon Father Rwagema played the recorded apparition Segatashya had of Jesus. I shivered as I remembered the thunder that roared across Kibeho after the boy told the Lord that the pilgrims needed a miracle to make them believe. I recalled how, even through the tiny speaker on the tape recorder, the force of God's reply rattled the windows in our church. *What miracle could top that?* I wondered.

That's when I heard the voice of Faustin, a neighbor who'd just returned from a pilgrimage with his family. "The sun danced across the sky right before my eyes," he told my parents. "It danced and changed into many colors, like a rainbow swirling in a glass circle, and then it became as gray and pale as the moon. There was suddenly another sun behind the first one, illuminating it. On the face of the moon was a giant Eucharist and chalice, and then the colors changed again—like a third sun had emerged that was red, green, and gold. And the face of the Virgin Mary appeared in the center of the sun, just as clear as day!"

My imagination ignited, setting my curiosity ablaze. I jumped from my bed and leaned toward the window to hear the adult conversation better. After hearing that Our Lady's face had appeared in the sun, I knew there was no way I'd be falling asleep.

"It's true," confirmed Faustin's wife, Béatrice. "The visionary Agnes was having an apparition of Jesus when everybody in the crowd started looking up at the sky. The nearest people to the podium looked up first and caused a chain reaction. It was strange seeing thousands of heads turn up, one after the other, like watching a stack of dominos toppling toward me.

"When *I* looked up, I thought I'd gone crazy. I blinked and rubbed my eyes, then blinked and rubbed again . . . the sun really was dancing. It moved back and forth as though God Himself were tossing it from one hand to the other. And then another sun emerged from the dancing light; there were two suns in the sky! They spun in circles of opposite direction: one spun clockwise and the other counterclockwise, but then they spun into each other, reuniting as a single sun."

I heard several gasps of astonishment in the yard, then a long silence I took as either wonderment or disbelief. As for me, I was in complete awe.

François, a friend of my dad's who was visiting from another village, joined the conversation by sharing a story from his first pilgrimage to Kibeho, during which the sun had transformed into a looking glass. "It was a perfectly round mirror that reflected the world back to us," he stated, "and we could see the thousand hills of Rwanda filling the sky. Agnes pointed toward heaven as Jesus spoke to her, and said, 'Behold what you see—are there any among you who can deny now that they have a sign? Watch closely and remember what you witness. Believe your eyes or deny what you are seeing. But I ask you only to tell the truth.'"

Faustin told two more stories about miracles in the sky witnessed by many during Agnes's apparition. One was when the sun became two distinct colors: "It divided evenly, like a horizontal line had been drawn across the center of its surface. The bottom part was a beautiful pale blue, and the top half was as white as milk. Agnes said, 'The white is the purity of God, a sign that He will soon return and we must prepare for His arrival. The blue is the love of the Blessed Mother shining on the world. The blue represents the color of Our Lady's clothing.'"

Our neighbor then described a miracle that happened later that same afternoon. He said that Agnes had abruptly stopped speaking while delivering a message and again pointed to heaven. "It was the greatest miracle I've seen," he insisted. "There, far above our heads, was an image of Jesus on the cross, with the Blessed Mother standing below him with her head bowed in grief. When I checked to see if others were witnessing the same scene, I saw 15,000 people dropping to their knees, many making the sign of the cross, as they looked to the sky through tears of love." Faustin relayed this with such emotion that I suspected he was weeping.

My parents and their guests continued swapping stories about miracles witnessed at Kibeho.

"What I think is *really* miraculous is the conversion of so many hearts in Kibeho," my father said. "Each time I travel there I'm amazed that everyone feels the same way I do—completely loved by the Blessed Mother. When you sense how deep her love is for us all, you're so happy that you can't help but forgive everyone who's ever wronged you in any way. I think that everyone who goes to Kibeho leaves with a new understanding about the meaning of life."

Then my mother said that for her, the greatest miracle was that none of the young visionaries had been injured, either by falling down so hard after an apparition or because of the doctors from the bishop's medical commission who climbed onto the podium to examine the girls in the middle of their visions. "I couldn't bear watching the way the doctors treated those poor girls!" she exclaimed in a pained voice. "At first the examinations seemed routine, even helpful—they used a stethoscope and listened to the girls' heartbeats and measured their blood pressure. But as the apparitions went on, the tests became more extreme. To me it looked like torture!

"They pinched the girls with pliers to see if they'd react, stuck them with needles, twisted their arms behind their backs, and pushed them so hard the poor children fell to the ground. One doctor, who was quite a big man, actually kneeled on top of one of the teenagers and bounced up and down on her chest! None of the girls seemed hurt in any way; they didn't even seem to notice what was being done to them. During all that terrible testing, the girls' faces continued to beam with love as they talked and sang. But, oh my Lord, even if those youngsters couldn't feel any pain . . . the way they tortured those poor girls!"

Mom took a breath and then continued. "All I could think was, *What if that was my daughter?* I can promise you that if I saw some doctor lay a hand like that on my Immaculée, I'd jump up on the podium and smack his face. I don't care how many thousands of people were watching. The Virgin Mary is a mother just like me, so she'd understand why I'd beat up the bishop's doctor," my mother said, with complete seriousness.

Everyone in the yard laughed at how worked up she'd become, and soon she was laughing with them. I smiled from my bedroom, proud and happy that my mom loved me so much. But I also had a deeper understanding of her concern for me and realized that she was never going to let me make the trip to Kibeho—at least not on her watch.

Chapter 13

The Mystical Journeys

The miraculous events in Kibeho also included the mystical journeys that three of the visionaries took with the Blessed Mother. These astral expeditions traversed time and space and presented the girls with the rarest of gifts: a glimpse of heaven and hell.

Perhaps fittingly, the first visionary to set out on one of these amazing voyages was the first one Mary had chosen to appear to, Alphonsine Mumureke.

During an apparition in the middle of March 1982, Our Lady invited Alphonsine to travel with her to a special place, and she accepted the invitation with delight. "Of course, my darling," the young seer answered, with the characteristic casualness she used when addressing the Queen of Heaven. "You know I'll follow you anywhere. Just tell me when to be ready, my dear, and I'll be waiting!"

It was to be an overnight trip, for which they'd leave late on the coming Saturday and return on Sunday. Alphonsine laughed with pleasure when she heard this and thanked the Blessed Virgin for not forgetting to give her a present—Sunday was the girl's 17th birthday, and she could spend eternity trying to imagine a more wonderful way to celebrate.

Mary cautioned Alphonsine that some risk would be involved, and she provided specific instructions for Alphonsine to relay to the school director. A short while later, the visionary was standing before the director issuing Mary's instruction. "Don't bury me; my body will look dead, and you'll think that I'm dead, but please don't bury me!" Alphonsine emphatically instructed the stunned director who, after witnessing four months of supernatural visitations, was sure nothing would ever surprise her again. But she was taken aback by the teenager's claim that the mother of God was dropping by the dormitory on Saturday to pick Alphonsine up for an excursion.

"Where did you say she was taking you?" the director asked.

"Heaven," Alphonsine answered. "At least I think we're going to heaven. Mom didn't say exactly, but I had the feeling when she was talking to me . . . she also said to tell you that even though my body will look dead, you shouldn't be frightened because I'll be fine. My body will be here, but I'll be away until Sunday."

The director nodded, promising her student that no one would be allowed to bury her, at least until after the weekend. Then she dismissed Alphonsine and sent for the school nurse to tell her that she'd be needed at the school all weekend. She also penned a note to the bishop who'd recently set up the Commission of Enquiry, whose goal was to study anything the visionaries might say or do that would qualify as supernatural in nature. The director assumed that a trip to heaven with the Virgin Mary would certainly qualify.

On Saturday a nun went to check in on Alphonsine when she failed to show up for the evening meal and found the girl lying in bed, fully clothed, in what looked like a deep sleep. Her hands were neatly folded over her chest with her fingers entwined. The nun tried to shake her in order to wake her up and was alarmed that she couldn't budge the girl an inch, even when she pushed using all her strength. She shouted as loudly as she could into Alphonsine's ear, but she didn't react in the slightest. The worried woman leaned over Alphonsine, positioning her ear right above her mouth, and listened carefully for several minutes. She jumped back and crossed herself before rushing off to tell the school director that Alphonsine Mumureke was dead.

The director sent the school nurse to the visionary's bedside and notified the rest of the staff to meet in the dorm. She then sent a girl to fetch Abbot Augustin Misago, a leading member of the Commission of Enquiry, before running to the dormitory herself. As the director looked at the waxen figure stretched out on Alphonsine's bed, she remembered the girl's words to her: "Don't bury me; my body will look dead, and you'll think that I'm dead, but please don't bury me!"

Alphonsine certainly did look dead. The nurse hovered over her, pressing a stethoscope to the girl's chest, while a visiting Red Cross official was probing Alphonsine's neck with his fingers to find a pulse. Soon the entire school administration was standing at the visionary's bedside, curious about her possible voyage, but also deeply concerned for her well-being.

Abbot Misago, who would one day become the bishop responsible for passing verdict on the authenticity of the Kibeho apparitions, arrived to watch the proceedings closely with two priests who'd accompanied him from the seminary. He noted that in the packed room, there was no shortage of eyewitnesses when the testing commenced.

The medical practitioners worked quickly to first ensure that Alphonsine had indeed not died, as the nun who found her had been convinced was the case. They concluded that the young woman *was* alive, but barely. Her pulse rate was impossibly slow, her blood pressure was low, and her breathing was virtually nonexistent. In fact, her chest rose and fell imperceptibly only once or twice a minute—just enough to supply the oxygen needed to support life.

Despite determining that Alphonsine was alive and seemingly well, everyone in the room felt that they were staring at a corpse. Four men tried rolling her onto her side, but they couldn't move her. They attempted to separate her hands, but no matter how hard they pulled, her fingers remained clasped together. Two more men joined the attempt—after all six had strained with all their might to lift the slim teenager from the bed, they gave up in frustration. Abbot Misago would later say that it was like trying to lift a 200-pound slab of granite. And the nurse insisted that Alphonsine's limbs were so immovably locked in position that if she hadn't been breathing, the nurse would have concluded rigor mortis had set in.

Further testing was done to assess the girl's reflexes and pain impulses: her skin was pinched, her hair was tugged, and needles were even stuck into her skin and beneath her fingernails. Her response was always the same: she didn't respond at all.

The conclusion was that Alphonsine had either entered a level of sleep so deep that it resembled a coma, or she truly was comatose. The adults in the room decided to take shifts watching over the catatonic teen throughout the night.

Eighteen hours after entering the deathlike sleep, Alphonsine awoke livelier than ever. Her eyes were sparkling, her muscles were relaxed, and her face glowed with all the health and happiness of a beloved youth. She also smiled broadly because it was her birthday.

Later she described her trip in private to members of the commission, but she also shared some highlights with her curious classmates. "The first place Mary took me was dark and very frightening," she began. "It was filled with shadows and groans of sadness and pain. She called it 'the Place of Despair,' where the road leading away from God's light ends. Our travels were many . . . we moved across the stars until we arrived in a place of golden light filled with happiness and laughter and songs sung by so many joyous voices that I thought the souls of all the people who once had lived were floating around singing praises to God.

"But as in the Place of Despair, I couldn't see anyone —I could only hear their voices. I asked Mary why she wouldn't let me see the people who were so happy.

"'You cannot see what is here while you are still living below,' she told me.

"But whoever those people were could see me. A young voice, too young for me to know if it was a boy or girl, cried out to me with such friendliness and love that

I felt like weeping. 'Alphonsine,' it sang out. 'It's you! It's Alphonsine of Kibeho, who has seen the Blessed Virgin! You are blessed! I was like you; I too could see and was persecuted for my visions. Have faith and confidence in the Blessed Mother, for she will protect you. . . .'

"Then my eyes opened and I was in my bed with the happiness of that place flowing through my body."

ANATHALIE WAS ALSO ESCORTED ON TOURS of the universe with Mary. The best known of these began after a five-hour-long apparition; when it ended and Anathalie collapsed to the ground, her limbs became frozen with the same rigidity Alphonsine had experienced. The visionary lay stiff and unmoving on the podium for the next seven hours, as priests and doctors from the Commission of Enquiry conducted the same series of tests they'd done on Alphonsine.

When Anathalie awoke, she was in a daze and was carried to her bed, where she remained silent for two days. But then she spoke, describing the surreal and glorious places the Holy Mother had taken her. The first was a world where instead of mountains, hills, and valleys, the landscape was comprised of varying shades of vivid color and light, and people traveled from place to place by sliding through the light.

Mary led Anathalie to one strange land illuminated only by white light. Here, the girl saw seven handsome men wearing white cloaks and standing in a circle, and they were creating the most beautiful music without any instruments—each note was filled with a different sensation of contentment and joy. She asked, "Where are we, Mother?"

"This is Isangano, the focal point; this is the place of communion."

"Who are those men?"

"They are not men. They are angels."

"What do they do here?"

"They praise God, watch over Earth, and aid humanity when they are needed or called upon."

Anathalie and the Queen of Heaven then floated to three different worlds, each of which was bathed in its own unique color and light, but the vividness of the color and intensity of the light diminished the farther they traveled from the angels.

At the next place the young lady saw millions of people dressed in white. All of them seemed overwhelmingly happy but not blissful, as the angels had been. "Our Lady told me that this was Isenderezwa z'ibyishimo, the place of the cherished of God," Anathalie explained.

"And then we moved on to our next destination, a world where the light was as dim as dusk. Below us were people dressed in clothes of dreary and duller colors in comparison to the other worlds we'd seen. Most of them seemed content, but many seemed quite sad and were even suffering. Mary said, 'This is Isesengurwa, a place of purification; the people you see are Intarambirwa, those who persevere.'

"The last place we visited was a land of twilight where the only illumination was an unpleasant shade of red that reminded me of congealed blood. The heat that rose from that world was stifling and dry—it brushed my face like a flame, and I feared that my skin would blister and crack. I couldn't look at the countless people who populated that unhappy place because their misery and anguish pained me so greatly. Mary didn't have to say the name of this place . . . I knew I was in hell.

"The next things I remember were someone laying me down in my bed and the Blessed Virgin above me, telling me to spend two days reflecting in silence on what I'd seen. 'Do not meditate on the angels you saw; they are not from this world,' she said, before explaining to me the nature of the other three places she'd shown me.

"The first place, the happy world of the cherished of God, was reserved for people whose hearts are good, who pray regularly, and who strive always to follow God's will.

"Our second visit to the place of purification was for those who called on God only during times of trouble, turning away from Him when their troubles were over.

"The last place of heat and no name was for those who never paid God any attention at all."

THE THIRD VISIONARY TO TRAVEL TO HEAVEN WAS VESTINE. I heard about her invitation on a Sunday morning while I was hurrying to get ready to go to Mass with my parents. I was smoothing the wrinkles out of my pretty white church dress when I heard a replay of the visionary's latest apparition. Her words made me toss the dress on my bed in a heap and sit down beside the radio. I knew I'd be in trouble for making my parents late for Mass, but this was *big!*

It seems that Jesus had asked Vestine to die for him on Good Friday, but he promised that she'd be resurrected on Easter Sunday. The request frightened and fascinated me. *Who would I be willing to die for?* I wondered. *My parents? My brothers? Would I let myself die for Jesus?* I couldn't answer my own question. Was there *anybody* I'd trust enough to believe if they said that they promised to give my life back to me tomorrow if I'd just agree to lie down and die today? Was I capable of the kind of love that such an act of faith required?

Everything inside of me was telling me that our Lord was using Vestine to give us an opportunity to question just how strong our faith really was—would it be strong enough for us to survive what lay ahead?

Our Savior had died for us, and now he was asking Vestine to die for him. I was sure that tens of thousands of Rwandans listening to the same broadcast were wondering if the young woman's faith was strong enough to vow, "Yes, I will die for you, and I know you will resurrect me." I was also sure that as they waited to hear Vestine's answer, they were asking themselves if *their* faith was strong enough, too.

"Yes, Jesus, I will die for you," Vestine said, an answer I believe bolstered the faith of all Rwandans. "Yes, I will do your will."

The son of God told the girl that while she was dead, he'd keep her soul in heaven. Vestine made sure to let everyone know not to bury her, even if a doctor signed a death certificate. She was going to die for Jesus on Good Friday at exactly 3 P.M., the hour Christ died on the cross, and be resurrected from the dead on Easter Sunday.

The countryside was astir with the news of Vestine's impending death and resurrection. "What does she mean when she says that she's going to die for Jesus?" my friend Jeanette asked me, totally confounded by the notion. "Does she mean that she'll pretend to die . . . that she's going to play dead for Jesus?"

"No, she isn't going to pretend," I answered, feeling a bit put off that Jeanette would even consider such a silly idea. "What would be the point in pretending to die? Jesus didn't!"

"So Vestine is really going to be dead, like she drowned or got eaten by a leopard?"

I hadn't considered the technical aspects of how the visionary would "die" because I was so wrapped up in the meaning of her sacrifice and the depth of her faith.

"How is she going to die?" Jeanette pressed me. "Will God strike her dead, or does somebody in Kibeho have to kill her?"

"No! Nobody is going to have to kill her, Jeanette!" I barked. Taking a moment to calm down, I thought hard about how Vestine's death might come about. "I think it will be like when Mary took Alphonsine to heaven," I said. "She'll just lie down on her bed, and Jesus will come and take her soul to heaven. And on Sunday he'll come back to Kibeho with Vestine's soul and put it back in her body."

"That makes sense," my friend agreed. "I guess if someone really wanted to, they could fake talking to Mary or Jesus. But I think it would be really hard to fake being dead."

Jeanette was right, and those investigating the visionaries were going to make certain that anything Vestine did over Easter weekend was supervised, tested, scrutinized, and documented. Journalists also descended on Kibeho to keep the country informed of her progress. With little else for them to report until the appointed time on Friday afternoon, they broadcast the arrivals of each member of the Commission of Enquiry; noted the doctors and nurses assigned to monitor Vestine's vital signs; described the medical equipment being carried into the building; and, of course, announced the arrival of Vestine herself.

At 3 P.M., Vestine winced as though seized by a sudden pain, and then she fell back on her bed, closed her eyes, and died.

The doctors were dumbfounded. The young woman had simply stopped breathing; they couldn't hear her heartbeat or detect her pulse; and it was noted that her blood pressure had dropped to zero. The results were checked and rechecked, but they remained the same. The doctors sat staring at her for more than an hour, trying to decide if they should pronounce her dead and announce publicly that Vestine Salima had passed away in her sleep.

Quite a debate between the theologians and the medical team ensued. From a strictly scientific perspective, she was dead; yet from the theological point of view, if she really had passed on, it was God's will and exactly what Jesus had said would happen—which means that she might also arise from the dead as he'd promised. Everybody decided to just sit tight.

Vestine took a long deep breath and exhaled with a small sigh. Other than the slight expansion of her rib cage as her lungs filled with air, there was no movement or sign of life. She continued taking a single deep breath every hour or two, which perplexed the doctors but convinced them that the young lady's body was functioning. She was gone, but she wasn't dead. All they could do was wait for Easter Sunday and see if Christ would indeed raise the visionary from the dead.

They waited 40 hours. Then, just after dawn on Easter Sunday, Vestine woke up. She rubbed the sleep from her eyes; stretched her arms toward the ceiling; and let out a long, relaxed yawn. She looked around the room at the exhausted team of investigators and doctors and smiled. "Good morning, everyone," she said cheerfully. "Happy Easter!"

She climbed out of bed, picked up her towel and soap, and headed off to wash up before morning Mass. The doctors stopped her, insisting that she let them do some basic tests, which she allowed. When everything came up as completely normal, the young woman tried to continue on her way to the washbasin—but everyone was shouting at her to tell them what had happened.

The visionary paused in the doorway for a moment, as though she were trying to recall what actually had transpired. "Jesus told me that I'd die on Friday afternoon and be resurrected on Sunday morning. And that's what happened," she said, and she left to wash and dress for Easter Mass.

Vestine made a point, as she always did, of greeting the priest after Mass, and he asked her about the marking on her face. She had no idea what he was talking about and was taken aback when she returned to her room and looked in the mirror: a cross had formed in the center of her forehead! She rubbed her hand over it, but it was part of her skin, like a birthmark or tattoo. The doctors examined it and said that the pigmentation on her skin had changed. When they couldn't offer a medical explanation, they reported to the theological commission that it was not a burn or bruise, and it was definitely not self-inflicted.

The investigators sat down with Vestine and asked her if she recalled anything during her 40 hours in which she was dead asleep.

"I can't describe it," she replied. "Jesus lifted me to heaven, but I can't describe it—I don't know how to. There were colors I'd never seen before and they sounded like music, and music like I'd never heard before that sounded like color. There are no words . . . I don't know how to explain the feeling of being there because I've never felt anything like it. How would I describe what it's like to breathe water or drink air? I couldn't, because it's impossible for me to do so. There's no way to compare heaven and Earth.

"But I can tell you this: I begged Jesus from the bottom of my soul to let me stay there. He said that it wasn't my time, so I must leave. There has never been a sadder moment for me."

"Then why were you so happy when you awoke?" one of the investigators asked.

"Because I know that I'll be going back to heaven, and when I do, I'll be able to stay forever."

Chapter 14

Mary's Tears
in a River of Blood

It was supposed to be a happy occasion, a celebration of the day the Holy Mother left this world and joined her son in the kingdom of heaven. The Feast of the Assumption of the Blessed Virgin always falls on August 15, and on that date in 1982, Mary had promised to appear in Kibeho.

More than 20,000 people turned out for the festivities, expecting to hear the visionaries sing joyous songs from heaven and share apparitions filled with love befitting the special day. The fields around the seers' podium looked like a great church picnic, particularly since thousands had brought along their young kids. Some of the boys and girls were ill; their parents were hoping for miraculous cures because it's said that on this day, the mother of God is especially receptive to prayers for children.

Other individuals were certain that Mary would make another miraculous appearance in the sky, perhaps standing at the pearly gates so that her earthly children could reflect on her entrance into paradise. Instead, what they were shown was hell on Earth.

The tone and energy of the apparitions that day seemed different from the start. When Alphonsine entered her state of ecstasy, her heart opened to Our Lady by offering her the song of welcome: "Tuje None Kugushima Mubyeyi Udahemuka" ("We Come Here to Thank You, Faithful Mother"). Yet she was cut off by the Holy Mother after just three words.

"I am too sad to hear my children sing," the Blessed Mother told her.

The young woman began to sing the song again to cheer her, but the Virgin stopped her again. Alphonsine started the song seven times, and seven times was told to stop. The girl was painfully distressed by this; the Virgin Mary loved to hear her children sing and had never before refused to listen.

The Commission of Enquiry would later interview Alphonsine and the other visionaries to document their conversations that day with the Blessed Mother. Alphonsine told them that when she asked Mary why she didn't want to hear her favorite songs, the Virgin's face became etched with pain, and her eyes filled with tears of grief. After many minutes of mournful silence, the Queen of Heaven began to openly weep.

"Why are you crying, darling?" Alphonsine asked Mary, frightened and concerned. "Why do you show me your tears? What do they mean, Mother? Your sadness hurts me; I should be the one crying, not you!"

The Virgin Mary responded by shedding even more tears.

"Mother, please!" Alphonsine begged. "Why don't you answer me? I can't bear to see you so upset . . . please don't cry! Oh, Mother, I can't even reach up to console you or dry your eyes. What has happened that makes you so sad? You won't let me sing to you and you refuse to talk to me. Please, Mother, I have never seen you cry before, and it terrifies me!"

At last Mary responded to the distraught teenager, asking her to sing a specific song. The 20,000 people listening to the visibly upset Alphonsine couldn't hear the Virgin's voice, but they hung on every word the visionary uttered. Now they heard her say, "Mother, I love to sing to you, but are you sure you want me to sing *that* song?"

The young lady apparently fulfilled Our Lady's request by singing "Naviriye ubusa mu Ijuru" ("I Came from Heaven for Nothing"):

> *People are not grateful,*
> *They don't love me,*
> *I came from heaven for nothing,*
> *I left all the good things there for nothing.*

> *My heart is full of sadness,*
> *My child, show me the love,*
> *You love me,*
> *Come closer to my heart.*

"Mother, you're still weeping . . . please tell me what's making you cry," Alphonsine said, abruptly ending the song. "Remember when you promised me that you'd give me anything I asked you for? Well, I'm asking this of you now: *Please don't cry!*"

Many minutes passed in silence as Alphonsine listened and received the message Mary wanted her to share. Then the girl said, "Yes, Mother, I will repeat it exactly as you ask me to. To the people on Earth, you say three times: You opened the door and they refused to come in. You opened the door and they refused to come in. You opened the door and they refused to come in. . . . Yes, Mother, I'm telling them you say that you saw the world in a bad state and you came to save us, but we've refused to listen.

"But Mother, we're only human. What can we do?" the visionary asked, and then listened intently to the response she received.

"Yes, I know," she continued. "But it's hard to make them understand. The words and songs you just told me to share are difficult for many to understand. Some grasp their meaning, but others don't. Some just won't listen!

"Mother, you should speak to the people yourself, for we are not wise enough to deliver your messages. When we tell folks what you ask us to say to them, they call us crazy—they say we've gone mad," Alphonsine went on. "Yes, I will continue to tell them. You want me to ask them three times: What are they waiting for? What are they waiting for? What are they waiting for?"

The Virgin then asked her to sing "The Queen of Heaven and Earth," a song she'd personally taught Alphonsine. The song's lyrics tell people how and why they must repent and pray, and Our Lady asked the visionary to repeat one phrase of the song seven times: *So we can help Jesus to save the world.*

Suddenly Alphonsine let out a gut-wrenching scream that cut through the startled crowd like a razor. "I see a river of blood! What does that mean? No, please! Why did you show me so much blood? Show me a clear stream of water, not this river of blood!" the seer cried out, as the Holy Mother revealed one horrifying vision after another. The young woman was subjected to so many images of destruction, torture, and savage human carnage that she pleaded, "Stop, stop, please stop! Why, Mother? Why are you showing me this? The trees are exploding into flames, the country is burning! Please, Mother, you're scaring me. . . . Oh no! *No!* Why are those people killing each other? Why do they chop each other? I'm not a strong enough person to watch people killing each other."

Tears gushed from Alphonsine's eyes as she trembled uncontrollably at the scenes unraveling before her. She summoned a hymn to her lips, trying to sing the images away, but she soon fell silent, as though frozen in fear. Mary was revealing even more dreadful images to her—for example, the girl was now staring at a growing pile of severed human heads, which were still gushing blood. The grotesque sight worsened still as Our Lady expanded Alphonsine's vision until she beheld a panoramic view of a vast valley piled high with the remains of a million rotting, headless corpses, and not a single soul was left alive to bury the dead.

The Blessed Mother was warning the crowd gathered in front of the visionary of the horror that awaited Rwanda. And she used imagery so graphic and gruesome that many parents fled Kibeho, carrying their traumatized children in their arms.

As the vision began to fade, Mary asked the stricken Alphonsine to sing another song, this time repeating two lines of verse seven times each:

First: *There will be fire that will come from beneath the earth and consume everything on Earth . . .*

And then: *The day you will come to take those who have served you, God, we beg you to have mercy on us . . .*

"How am I supposed to sleep tonight after you

showed me all those horrible things?" the young woman wailed. "How will I ever sleep again?"

Alphonsine then prayed that what she'd been shown would never come to pass, not in Rwanda or anywhere in God's world. She prayed for all the people she knew, and then for all the people she didn't know, asking Jesus to shelter them from such evil. She sang one more song pleading for Christ to be merciful and forgive sinners, and then she collapsed on the podium.

ALPHONSINE'S GHASTLY APPARITION HAD SHAKEN the thousands who'd listened to her describe such unspeakable horrors, and they tried to imagine a troubled land where such horrors could come to pass.

But as visionary after visionary stepped onto the podium that day, each received the same images from the weeping Virgin. For hours their horrified cries echoed through the hills, describing rivers of blood, savage murders, and the putrefying remains of hundreds of thousands of people. For some it must have seemed terrifyingly obvious that the seers were speaking about Rwanda.

The images were a cautionary glimpse into the near future for the more than 20,000 people gathered in Kibeho that day, who were warned again and again that the hatred they harbored in their hearts toward their neighbors would lead them to ruin.

Marie-Claire continually wailed at the images she was shown, and she begged Rwandans to heed Mary's pleas and warnings before it was too late: "Our Lady says, 'Do not forget that God is more powerful than all the evil in the world . . . the world is on the edge of catastrophe. Cleanse your hearts through prayer. The only way is God. If you don't take refuge in God, where will you go to hide when the fire has spread everywhere?'"

Unfortunately, not enough people prayed—too few cleansed their hearts of hatred.

The fire did indeed come, and there was nowhere to hide for more than a million innocent souls whose bodies were chopped to pieces during the genocide that engulfed Rwanda in the spring of 1994. Thousands upon thousands of bodies were dumped into rivers that ran thick with human blood. Alphonsine's apocalyptic vision was so horrifically accurate that Mary's messages would eventually be believed and accepted by everyone from the peasants to the Pope.

But by that time, it was too late.

Chapter 15

Mary, above Kibeho and Throughout History

By the mid-1980s some of the visionaries' apparitions had ended or were becoming less frequent: Marie-Claire's lasted only six months, until September 1982; Anathalie's (at least her public ones) ended in late 1983; and Alphonsine received visits from Our Lady until 1989, but usually just once a year on the anniversary of their first meeting, November 28. However, Mary and Jesus continued visiting the other seers for many months and years.

Radio Rwanda continued to air the apparitions, but the government-run station greatly reduced its coverage of Kibeho when visionaries began delivering messages critical of the extremist Hutu government's discrimination against the minority Tutsi tribe.

One of their policies included limiting the number of Tutsi children, like me, allowed to attend federally funded high schools, which were vastly superior to private schools. Even though I had some of the highest marks in the region, my ethnic background blocked me from advancing in school and ever finding a career. So being denied access to the public education system devastated me.

Thankfully my parents could manage to send me to board at a private high school, but such facilities were far inferior and not as highly regarded in Rwanda. The school I moved to in 1985 was no exception: There was no running water or electricity, books were scarce, and there was little to no equipment to use in science classes. Discipline was lax, and academic standards weren't as high as they were in the schools funded by the government. In short, this wasn't a place from which the national college would be accepting applicants.

Still, for two years I studied hard to keep up my grades, and I faithfully asked God through prayer to provide me with a higher education. I also entreated Mary to put in a good word for me because I knew that Jesus loved his mother so much he could never refuse anything she requested. As always, the Virgin heard my prayers.

One day my classmate Valerie announced that her brother had just returned from Kibeho, where the visionary Valentine Nyiramukiza had said the Holy Mother would make a special blessing for those who wanted to go to Kibeho but couldn't make the pilgrimage. "Our Lady calls them her faithful 'pilgrims of the heart,' and she had a message for them," Valerie told us.

Oh, my God! It's a message for me! I thought, my heart skipping.

"She asked all her pilgrims of the heart to look in the sky toward Kibeho at midnight tomorrow to see a sign from her. When we see it, we're to ask for her blessing and then say a special prayer if we have a wish we need fulfilled or a dream we want to come true."

Hearing this, we all went crazy. We'd heard such visions described by pilgrims who'd returned from Kibeho, but we'd never seen one firsthand. None of us had ever even been allowed to go to Kibeho, and this was our chance to witness a miracle ourselves!

It was too scary to go outside at night, so we planned to meet in front of the only dormitory window facing south toward Kibeho. And dozens of us—Catholic, Protestant, and Muslim girls alike—had shown up, all hoping for Mary to appear. Rumors spread that the sign might appear as soon as sunset, so we assembled at the window at 7 P.M., five hours ahead of schedule, just in case the Holy Virgin did show up early. As we crowded around that window, we sang our favorite song to her:

Mary is the mother of God,
The kindest mother ever to be.
Mary is the star that shines to guide,
All those who are lost at sea.

We placed a windup travel clock on the windowsill and waited for a miracle as the hours ticked by.

Every ten minutes or so a girl would shout out, "There she is! She's a dove . . . Mary has come to us as a dove!" Or, "Look, it's a sign of the cross!" But when we'd examine it more closely, it would turn out to be nothing.

After a few hours many of my schoolmates grew weary and drifted off to bed. But not me—I stood at that window and stared into the endless depths of God's spiraling galaxies. *That's what eternity must look like,* I thought, remembering my science teacher explaining how the light from every star travels millions of miles for millions of years just to shine above Rwanda.

By midnight, there were about 20 girls left at the window when the sky began to change. At first I didn't believe my eyes, but the harder I looked, the more certain I was that a group of stars in the southern sky was becoming brighter by the second. The light emanating from these stars had a bluish tinge that soon shone so brilliantly it dwarfed the nearby constellations. And that's when the starlight formed an unmistakable image: a profile of the Virgin Mary, with her hands folded before her in prayer.

As the other girls were screaming out in disbelief and wonder, tears rolled down my face. I smiled, made the sign of the cross, and whispered my special prayer to the Queen of Heaven.

Ten minutes later the stars had faded—the mother of God was gone from the sky but not from our hearts. No matter what religion the girls who'd stood with me that night at the window belonged to, they were changed forever.

That starry image of Mary blazing in the sky was burned permanently into my mind. After that event I always knew the Blessed Mother was a part of the cosmos, eternally above and always watching over me. And while I don't know how many of the girls made a special prayer that night, or if their prayers were answered, I do know that mine was.

Not long after I went home for summer vacation, I found out that I'd been accepted at Lycée de Notre Dame d'Afrique. Lycée was one of the best public high schools in the country, and most of its graduates went on to university.

That night, my entire family was overjoyed and celebrated together. That was when my father told me that he'd taken Marie-Claire's words to heart—that we can obtain anything by praying for it faithfully. After he told me that he'd asked Mary to help me get into a high school that would pave my way to university, I admitted that my special prayer had been for the exact same thing. We both smiled.

"Imagine what the world would be like if we all prayed to Our Lady with faith and love," Dad said.

DURING MY THREE YEARS STUDYING AT LYCÉE, I had many wonderful experiences. One of the greatest of these was meeting Sarah, who became such a dear friend that her parents took me in and sheltered me after the genocide. But in those more carefree days at school, we enjoyed visiting each other's homes, and my very first trip to hers changed my life.

Toward the end of our summer vacation in 1988, Sarah first invited me to come to her house in Kigali to see the "big city" before school started. My dad agreed to drive me from Mataba, a trip that would take several hours. Fortunately, we received some wonderful news before we left that occupied us for the entire journey.

On August 15, during the annual Feast of the Assumption, Bishop Jean-Baptiste Gahamanyi had announced his authorization of public devotion at the apparition site in Kibeho. My father and I couldn't talk about anything else.

"Does this mean that the Church believes Mary and Jesus are really appearing in Kibeho? Are they going to build the chapel and the basilica the way Our Lady told Anathalie she wanted it built?" I asked excitedly, picturing what the basilica would look like perched atop the hill in Kibeho. *Like the castle of God,* I thought.

"No, Immaculée, you're getting way ahead of yourself. Calm down a bit."

"Then they *don't* believe they're appearing?"

"What it means is that Bishop Gahamanyi does believe that Mary and Jesus are appearing at Kibeho, but he wants to be sure and gather enough proof to convince the Vatican. His Commission of Enquiry has been working for six years now, and he thinks they've got enough information on the visionaries to start making a decision. All the evidence the bishop has looked at so far seems to prove that the apparitions are real, and he doesn't think people should have to wait for a final decision—they should go to Kibeho and worship as soon and as often as they want and know they have the Church's blessing," Dad clarified.

"So that means we can go?"

"Not just yet. Let's wait until you're out of school or at university, and then we can go. Kibeho isn't going anywhere."

I'd been resigned for a long time to the fact that even if my father agreed to take me to Kibeho, my mother would never let him. I was going to have to wait until I was old enough to go on my own. "What about Our Lady's chapel and the basilica? Are they going to start building them right away?" I asked him now.

"Not until the apparitions have been fully approved, and even then it could take years and years. The basilica Anathalie described sounds like it's going to be bigger than all of Mataba, and they don't even have a decent road in Kibeho yet!"

Despite what Dad said, by the time we got to Kigali, I was certain that one day there would be a chapel for

Our Lady of Kibeho and a basilica on top of the hill. After I got to Sarah's house, she and I spent many hours planning a future trip when we could go by ourselves. We were sure that the basilica would have thousands of luxurious guest rooms so that the pilgrims wouldn't have to sleep outside on the ground anymore or have to walk to a river to take a bath or get a drink of water.

"Kibeho will be as famous as Fátima and Lourdes, don't you think, Immaculée?" Sarah asked.

"Definitely *more* famous," I answered. "We've got way more visionaries than they ever had! People will come from all over the world to pray in Kibeho."

"Well, until they build the basilica here, I'd have to say that Lourdes is my favorite apparition site," my friend said. "What's yours?"

"I can't decide. I like Lourdes just as much as Fátima; Our Lady was so beautiful at both places."

"Well, you don't just have to choose between Fátima and Lourdes . . . what are your five favorites?"

"What do you mean, *five?*" I asked, confused. "Mary has only appeared at Fátima and Lourdes—"

"I can't believe it!" Sarah broke in with a laugh. "Except for my mother, I've never met anyone who loves the Blessed Mother more than you do, and you've only heard about Fátima and Lourdes! Wait here, Immaculée. I've got a present for you that you're going to love."

My friend came back a few minutes later with a big smile on her face and placed a large blue book on my lap. The color on the old volume's cover was quite faded, but the title embossed upon it in striking gold lettering left me speechless: *Marian Apparitions Throughout History.* Sarah laughed again at my reaction.

In the years since Miss Odette had first told me about Fátima and Lourdes, no one had mentioned any other appearances of Our Lady to me. I couldn't believe that my parents and priest didn't know anything about the subject . . . or that I'd never asked. But in a country where half the people couldn't spell their own names, there weren't many books in public circulation. Of course since Sarah's parents lived in the capital city of Kigali, imported books would be more common than they were in my rural village.

Yet where the book came from didn't matter; where it would take me was the important part.

I EAGERLY READ *MARIAN APPARITIONS THROUGHOUT HISTORY* night after night in my dorm room, and each page held a new revelation. I found that the Holy Mother's love for her children is truly eternal—she's been appearing to people on Earth for nearly 2,000 years!

It turns out that the first apparition of the Virgin Mary ever recorded was to St. James the Greater, who was the brother of John, the beloved disciple of Jesus. James was preaching in Spain in the year A.D. 40, and it's believed that Mary was still alive then! The book said that she appeared as a flesh-and-blood woman but descended from the sky on a pillar carried by angels and told James, "Here on this ground you will build my house and use this pillar for my temple." James did as Mary asked and built a church there in the place now known as Zaragoza. Even today, centuries and centuries later, people still make pilgrimages to Zaragoza because there have been so many miraculous cures and healings there.

As I read on I discovered that, just as she'd done in Kibeho, the Blessed Virgin often told visionaries that she wanted a chapel or shrine to be built on the site where she appeared so people could pray there. And her messages all over the world were often the same as they were in Kibeho: love each other, have faith in God, pray to her to find comfort, and allow her to lead the way to her son's merciful love.

Hundreds of visitations have been reported and investigated through the centuries, but only a relative few have been recognized by the Church. Two that were recognized were my beloved Fátima and Lourdes, but the book introduced me to a new favorite: Our Lady of Guadalupe in Mexico. I loved this story because it showed how the power of Mary's love can lead thousands of hearts to conversion.

The story of Our Lady of Guadalupe began on December 9, 1531, when she appeared to a 57-year-old peasant named Juan Diego as he hiked along Tepeyac Hill just outside Mexico City. Born an Aztec, this man grew up in a culture where tens of thousands of people were sacrificed to pagan gods every year; in fact, when Juan was just 13 years old, 80,000 human sacrifices were made in four days to consecrate a pyramid.

Juan Diego had only recently been baptized into the Christian faith when a lady appeared to him in the form of a teenage girl, who said that she was the "Mother of the true God who gives life." She then told Juan that she wanted a church built on Tepeyac Hill and instructed him to inform the local bishop of her wishes. Of course the bishop didn't believe the peasant and sent him away.

Juan returned to his home that night to find that his uncle, whom he loved very much, was gravely ill and about to die. The next day, the poor man was supposed to meet back with the lady to talk about the bishop's reaction, but instead he went to fetch a priest to administer the last rites to his uncle. He tried to hide from her by sneaking around Tepeyac Hill, but she intercepted him.

"Where are you going, my son?" the lady asked gently.

Juan was greatly ashamed and begged her to find another messenger because he was not worthy. He bowed before her and begged her forgiveness. "I'm so sorry," he said. "My uncle who loves the Lord is dying, and I was going to get a priest to take his last confession. Please forgive me for deceiving you; I was so worried for my uncle's soul and had to hurry."

After listening to Juan's heartfelt apology, the lady answered him with the kindness of a loving mother: "My child, do not be afraid of me and do not grieve for your uncle. Do not be frightened of sickness or death. Am I not here? Am I not your mother? Are you not my cherished child, whom I will shield against all harmful things? Do you not feel protected in the cloak of my presence? Put your heart to rest, for you have no need to fear when I am with you. Your uncle will not die from the sickness that grieves you—he has been cured."

As Juan would later learn, his uncle had been cured the very moment the lady spoke those words. But right now, his heart was eased by her gentle words, and he told her how the bishop had sent him away. She merely sent him back to repeat her message.

Before the bishop sent Juan away again, he told the peasant to offer him proof of the lady's appearance by bringing him a sign that would convince him. When Juan related this to her, she chose to send a sign in the form of a type of rose that was difficult to find and never grew at that time of year. She provided Juan with the blooms, which he wrapped in his "tilma" (a type of cape made of cactus fiber) and took to the bishop.

When Juan Diego unwrapped his tilma in front of the bishop, the holy man didn't just see the roses—he also witnessed a beautiful image of the Virgin Mary emblazoned on the peasant's cape. The bishop broke into tears, fell to his knees, and asked the Blessed Mother's forgiveness for his disbelief. He carefully draped the tilma on the altar and then immediately ordered the construction of a shrine exactly where the mother of God had requested.

When the story of Juan's visitation and the Holy Virgin's image on his tilma spread through the Aztec people, human sacrifices ended immediately. Within a decade, nine million people had also converted to Christianity, the largest single conversion in Christian history.

Today, the church the bishop built for Mary has become the Basilica of Our Lady of Guadalupe, and more than 15 million individuals go there every year to pray at her shrine. In addition, they stare in wonder at her beautiful image on Juan's tilma, which after nearly 500 years has remained miraculously intact—defying scores of scientific tests that have tried to account for the miracle. Thousands of men, women, and children are cured of all manner of physical and mental illness every year when they look upon Our Lady's image on that tilma.

After reading the book Sarah gave me, I knew that Mary was, and always would be, the Blessed Mother of the entire world and has appeared everywhere on the planet with messages of love for her children. Perhaps our little podium in a rural African village would one day be as well known as the other apparition sites and lead to the conversion of millions of hearts.

Chapter 16

Mary, Through Happiness, Heartache, and Horror

It dawned on me that if I was going to help make Our Lady of Kibeho known to the world, then I'd better get to that village myself at least once in my lifetime. My first opportunity to make a pilgrimage came when I was accepted into the National University in Butare (with the Holy Virgin's help, of course). One of the prayer groups there had arranged a bus trip to Kibeho, a drive of several hours. Of course it wasn't quite the same as the long pilgrimage my father had made on foot for many days, which was a huge part of his experience. Still, this was my moment—my opportunity to make the journey I'd been praying to go on for so many years. So I gratefully hopped on that bus and, with 40 other students, sang and clapped the entire way.

Unfortunately, my first trip to Kibeho was a complete disaster. My boyfriend, John, who wasn't Catholic or a huge fan of the Virgin Mary, had accepted my invitation to join me in what I was sure would be a life-changing journey. As the bus pulled into the parking area of Kibeho High School, I saw a huge crowd gathered in front of the podium, where the visionary Valentine was leading everyone in song.

Everyone on the bus poured out of it and rushed to join the throng of singing and dancing pilgrims. I had only taken a few steps toward the stage when Valentine's apparition began and she dropped to her knees. The crowd fell silent . . . this was it!

I was just about to run toward the podium when John grabbed my arm and stopped me. "We have to get out of here!" he said in a panicky voice. My boyfriend tended to be a very easygoing fellow, and I'd never seen him this upset.

"What are you talking about? We just got here!"

"I mean it, Immaculée," he insisted. "There's a bus leaving over there, and we're getting on it." He took my hand and, before I knew it, we were in front of the departing vehicle.

"John, stop! Do you know how long I've waited to come to Kibeho? You better have a pretty good reason for wanting me to leave!" We were standing beside the bus's open door, and the driver was looking down at us impatiently as he tapped the gas pedal with his foot. I had to shout over the revving engine. "If this is a Catholic/Protestant thing, you know that doesn't matter to me. Mary loves all of us, and she's gentle and kind . . . what on earth are you so frightened about?"

"I'm not frightened!" he snapped, his male pride a bit wounded. "I'm sick, that's all. I suddenly don't feel very well, and I must go home. You can stay or go, but I'm leaving." He climbed aboard, and I dutifully followed behind him. If he really was ill, it would be pretty callous of me not to care for him on the long ride back. After all, the Blessed Mother had told us repeatedly to care for the sick and comfort each other.

This is what Mary wants me to do, I thought, sitting down beside my loved one as Kibeho disappeared behind me. Yet I couldn't help but note, *I finally make my first trip to this sacred place, and I never made it out of the parking lot!*

On the way back to campus, John offered me no explanation for his behavior, and he seemed in fine health once we were down the road a bit. I felt as if I'd just tossed away a ticket to heaven; there was a painful knot in my stomach, and I wanted to break into tears.

It turns out that John's "sickness" was a guilty conscience. A few days later he confessed that he'd been unfaithful to me one time in a moment of weakness, and he felt terrible about it. "When I set foot on the ground at Kibeho, I was overwhelmed with remorse," he told me. "I could feel Mary looking right into my soul . . . I swear she knew my heart and every sin I'd ever committed. I was ashamed and thought that if we stayed, she'd tell the visionary about the mistake I made with that other woman and announce it to everyone over the loudspeaker. I didn't want you to find out about it that way—I thought you'd break up with me, and that's why we had to leave. Please forgive me, Immaculée."

Naturally, I was upset, but I was even more convinced that Mary touches all of our hearts. "Ask the Blessed Mother to forgive you, John. We were supposed to be chaste!" I cried, feeling my heart break for the first time. "Now that you've confessed to me, go and confess to the Holy Virgin. Remember that she told Agnes we must live with a pure heart *and* a pure body. Think about that when you go to Our Lady.

"Pray to God for forgiveness as well," I added. "And when you do, you better mean it from the bottom of your heart. Once you've asked to be forgiven by Mary and God, we'll have our own discussion about forgiveness."

JOHN AND I DIDN'T TALK MUCH BEFORE my next opportunity to go to Kibeho came weeks later. This time there was no turning back for me—as soon as my bus arrived in the early afternoon, the music and singing drew me through the crowd and toward the podium like a magnet.

Valentine was there again, with several journalists at her feet recording her every word. As she sang some of Our Lady's favorite songs, we all joined in. My heart had never felt lighter; it was as though invisible angels were lifting everyone off the ground so that we could float above our problems and woes while with the Blessed Mother.

The visionary's messages from Mary were mainly about forgiving others, which struck a chord in my heart, given my personal anger with John. I knew that if he'd asked for God's forgiveness, I'd forgive him, too, for both of our sakes.

"Our Lady says, 'My children, you must love each other and not hold on to anger,'" Valentine shared. "'Many in this country have hatred in their hearts; you must cleanse your own heart with my son's love. Pray, children—pray to me, and I will help you. A small seed of anger can grow into a great tree of hatred that can block God's light and cast you into darkness.

"'My children, please listen. You must grant forgiveness for the sins of others and pardon those who have hurt you. Remember how much I love you, and love others the same way.'"

Toward the end of the apparition, Mary asked Valentine to water her flowers, which is how the Blessed Mother often referred to those in the crowd. This was a wonderful time during the apparitions when the Virgin would guide the visionary through the thousands of pilgrims, granting benedictions to all, but also offering a lucky few a personal blessing with holy water.

Valentine descended from the podium with a bottle of water, never taking her eyes away from the sky, where the Queen of Heaven floated above her. Everyone began singing and dancing with great joy, feeling the presence of the Holy Mother among us. Valentine, still looking at Mary and never making eye contact with us, would sprinkle a person with the water blessed by the Virgin and then move on until she was told to stop again.

As the seer drew closer, I prayed that she'd stop beside me. If she splashed me with holy water, I'd know that the Blessed Mother herself was hovering above me and bestowing me with her blessing.

There were lots of people around Valentine, some of whom were pursuing her with microphones and cassette recorders in an attempt to capture the blessings on tape, while others were begging for a personal message from the Virgin. Still others walked beside the visionary with extra containers of holy water to replace the one she carried if it emptied; they'd quickly put a container into her cupped hands because the young lady would never look down or break eye contact with Mary.

Valentine finally reached the spot where I was standing and stopped. She was so close I could have reached out and dipped my fingers in the water she held. But a blessing couldn't be stolen, especially right in front of the mother of God! I had to be patient and wait to see if

Our Lady would grace me with a benediction. My heart sank when Valentine started walking again and then passed by me. But she'd only gone a few yards when she stopped, turned around, and walked back to me. We stood face to face, with her looking up at the sky and seeing Mary, and me looking up at the sky and seeing . . . the sky. But I could feel the Blessed Mother there and was trembling with excitement.

Valentine was nodding her head, as if to say yes to the Virgin. Then she cupped her hand and filled it with holy water, nodded again, and lifted her hand to my lips without ever looking at me.

As I drank, I felt the water flow through my blood with the warmth of a mother's hug, which it was. Mary had just embraced me, and I knew that no matter what occurred in my life, that love would always be inside of me—no one would ever be able to take it from me. I'd been blessed.

I MADE THE PILGRIMAGE TO KIBEHO SEVERAL MORE TIMES over the next few years, and something wonderful always seemed to happen. Sometimes I'd even be privy to a minor miracle—such as the one I call "the Miracle of the Exam."

During my third year at university, I was walking to class when I passed a bus filled with students about to head off for Kibeho. *Too bad today is my busy day of classes, and they're all too important to miss,* I mused, watching the last few students get on the bus.

And it's too bad I have that major science exam tomorrow at 8 A.M. that's worth 70 percent of my term mark, I thought, as the doors of the yellow school bus hissed and closed.

But it would <u>really</u> be too bad if I didn't go and see the Holy Mother right now!

I banged on the door as the bus was pulling away. I didn't even wait for it to come to a complete stop before I leaped on board, sat in the one remaining free seat, and found myself headed to Kibeho. I had to be crazy, since I absolutely should have stayed on campus that day. Failing that exam could have cost me my scholarship; the consequences could be that horrendous. But Our Lady had tugged at my heart, so I followed her. I sensed she wanted me in Kibeho—and if she wanted me there, I'd put everything in her hands and stop worrying because she'd take care of me.

When I arrived, I noticed that there was a true celebration of Mary's love happening, with even more singing and dancing than usual. Valentine was on the podium, and we all quieted down when the apparition began. When the seer came out to water "her flowers" later on and passed me by, it didn't bother me at all, since the one drink I'd been given would last a lifetime.

A nun standing nearby was terribly disappointed she didn't stop, though, and I heard her complain, "Why does she never give me a blessing? I love the Blessed Mother so much, and I'm here so often, but I'm never given a blessing."

By that time Valentine was long gone and at the far side of the hill. I began dancing and singing with the other 10,000 pilgrims, and then I saw that she'd circled around and was standing behind me, beside the nun. The visionary's eyes were practically rolled up in her head while keeping total focus on the Blessed Virgin above her. She stood by the nun, nodded to Mary, said, "Blessings do not only come from water," and walked on. Everyone standing nearby was thrilled—Our Lady's gentle rebuke of the nun was an acknowledgment that Mary was watching over her, and that was truly a blessing.

Valentine moved up the stairs to the podium again and looked as though she was about to collapse, as she did at the end of every apparition. And she did collapse, but not before delivering one last message from the Virgin: "Many of you ran away from your duties of work and school today so that you could be with me. Because you came to see your mother, your mother will take care of you. You will not suffer for being here; I shall intercede on your behalf."

The next morning I was in the exam room waiting anxiously to see which of the 20 questions I could have been asked was the one that had been selected. Since I'd only had time to study for a single question beforehand, I figured I was doomed. When the clock struck eight, and I opened the booklet, I saw that the question I'd studied for was indeed the one on the exam. *Thank you, Mother,* I thought, as I put my pen to the paper and started to write. Of the 94 students who took that exam, only 2 passed . . . and I was one of them.

Sadly, the next time I heard Valentine's voice, it wasn't while I was celebrating with thousands of other happy, loving pilgrims—it was during the agonizing death throes of my compatriots. By that time those loving pilgrims were either killing or being killed by one another, and I was hiding in the bathroom of a local pastor with seven other women as the genocide raged around us.

I've written in my earlier books about those dark days, when all I could hear from my hiding spot were the screams of my neighbors and friends being slaughtered by people I'd known and trusted my entire life.

The sheer scale of murder, torture, and rape that swept through my country in the spring of 1994 would not have been possible if a lingering hatred hadn't been hiding in people's hearts. How many times had I heard Alphonsine, Marie-Claire, Anathalie, Segatashya, and all the other visionaries warn us that we were on the edge of disaster and that the hatred in our hearts would lead us to ruin? The Blessed Mother had been right: the seeds of an ethnic hatred hadn't been purged through prayer but had grown in a tree of death that had blotted out God's light and let unspeakable evil loose upon our land.

ALL THE WEEKS I HID IN THAT BATHROOM, I could hear the killers searching for me every day. From where I crouched I could hear scores of murders being committed only yards away from me. In the squalid, tiny room where those seven women and I huddled for our lives, we had no contact with the outside world. We knew only that there was a wholesale slaughter of the Tutsi tribe across the country and that we could be murdered at any moment.

I struggled with the hatred that filled my heart during this time, and I had to fight very hard to hold on to my faith in God. One day the brave pastor who was hiding us whispered to us through a crack in the bathroom door that the human carnage outside was so unthinkable that, even if we did survive the genocide, everyone we'd ever loved would surely be dead. It was my moment of deepest despair, and I was ready to turn away from a seemingly uncaring God as the fate of my family gnawed at me.

But that day Radio Rwanda, which had been broadcasting weeks of hate programming to encourage the killers, carried a live apparition from Kibeho. From somewhere inside the house we could hear every word of that broadcast, in which the visionary Valentine was communicating with the Blessed Mother. Hearing this message, which Mary delivered to me in the darkness of that room, made it possible for her to pierce the growing darkness in my soul:

> The gates of heaven are open, and your brothers and sisters are with me tonight. Do not cry for the ones you have lost; cry for those who are left behind. They will carry the suffering of what they have done, while those who have perished are in paradise tonight. Keep fighting; you will win. I am with you still, children. Have faith.

Those words comforted me like no others ever had. If my family had indeed been lost, then they were in the arms of the Blessed Mother, who was still reaching out from Kibeho to tell me that I was loved. She was still telling me to hold on to my faith. The love that flowed through me when I'd received Our Lady's blessing while drinking the water from Valentine's cupped hand warmed me again. My heart thirsted for God, and Mary quenched that thirst, leading me to my saving grace.

The Holy Virgin had given me the strength I needed to pray to God, and He found me. The bond of love I forged with Him in the weeks and months that followed have sustained me for the past 15 years, carrying me from terrible suffering and sorrow to happiness and peace.

Tragically, the very words Mary said that touched me so deeply were twisted and distorted by evil men who used Valentine's apparition as genocidal propaganda. The Blessed Mother had encouraged us to fight against spiritual darkness to win the freedom of God, reminding us that she was with us. But the killers said that she meant for them to continue their fight—a fight that was nothing more than a ruthless slaughter of Our Lady's helpless children.

During her next apparition, the Blessed Mother told Valentine that she was wounded deeply because the wicked had misused her words and harmed her children. The young lady soon left the country in despair.

THE EVIL THAT TORE THROUGH RWANDA didn't pass by Kibeho. More than 25,000 people were slaughtered where pilgrims once knelt in prayer to the Virgin, their bodies dumped into mass graves, soaking the sacred ground with innocent blood.

The horror also claimed the lives of several visionaries:

— Marie-Claire, who'd married and moved to Kigali in 1987 to teach, ran to the aid of her husband when killers were dragging him away. The murderers then turned on Marie-Claire, the feisty woman who once challenged the Holy Mother to a fistfight, and she was slain on the spot.

— Segatashya, the illiterate pagan boy Jesus plucked from a bean field and transformed into an eloquent preacher, was shot in the head by a death squad.

— Stephanie, the youngest of all of Mary's visionaries, disappeared during the holocaust and has never been heard from again.

After the genocide, the horrors predicted by Our Lady during the Feast of the Assumption in 1982 continued to haunt Kibeho. More than 200,000 refugees sought shelter on the very spot where Mary once spoke with such love. But the camp was infiltrated by killers hiding from government soldiers; in the ensuing battles, thousands of innocent victims were killed in the cross fire, trampled to death in the mayhem, or deliberately slaughtered as they fled.

After the carnage, bloodshed, and terror that devastated the village during and after the holocaust, the government closed down the apparition site and forbade public devotion to continue. It appeared that one of the most remarkable sites of Marian apparitions in history was going to be lost to the history of violence.

The remaining five visionaries were forced to move on with their lives, each working for the Lord in her own fashion:

— Alphonsine, the first of Mary's chosen messengers, became a cloistered nun in the Saint Claire convent of Abidjan, the capital of the Ivory Coast, and has since moved to the republic of Benin. She took the name "Alphonsine de la Croix Glorieuse," which means "Alphonsine of the Glorious Cross."

— After leaving Rwanda, Valentine ministered in several African countries before settling in Belgium, where she still receives public apparitions of Mary that hundreds of pilgrims attend. (In Kibeho, the Blessed Mother told Valentine that she'd be the last of the Rwandan visionaries to receive apparitions.)

— Agnes is married and now lives in Butare, where she's raising two children and is reportedly still receiving visitations from Jesus, whose messages she shares with her community.

— Vestine, who traveled with her staff for thousands of miles across Africa preaching God's word, survived the genocide but became ill soon afterward and passed away.

— And Anathalie, the second of the original three seers, has remained in Kibeho, fulfilling the promise she made to the mother of God more than 25 years ago. She leads a humble life of piety and prayer and works tirelessly to bring lost souls back to God's light. She helps out in the parish, where she faithfully and patiently answers the questions of hundreds of pilgrims and reporters. The Holy Virgin asked her to remain in Kibeho to pray and offer her suffering, and Anathalie told me that unless Our Lady tells her to, she will never leave.

AFTER KIBEHO HAD BEEN CLOSED OFF TO PILGRIMS for two years, the government decided to reopen it. It turns out that so many Rwandans were suffering so terribly that they begged those in charge to let them see the only mother they had left and seek her comfort. I was one of them, and I eagerly made my way back to the sacred site.

The road to Kibeho had never been good, but after the war, the deep ruts that had been cut in by military vehicles and the huge holes left from shelling and land mines made for an especially hellish ride. The village itself looked desolate, and the hills had been denuded by the 200,000 refugees who'd foraged there for months, looking for firewood or any food they could dig out of the ground.

Kibeho High School was a sad sight as well, for it was

riddled with bullets and boarded up. While the podium was still there, it was rotted and smashed. And as for the statue of the Blessed Virgin that looked over it all, her folded, praying hands had been shot off, and a bullet left a deep hole in her heart.

As tragic and sad as everything looked, I still felt Our Lady's presence. I continued to visit Kibeho whenever I could, and my heart lifted every time I was there. *Thank you for welcoming my parents and two brothers into your arms, Mother. Hold them close until we're together again,* I'd pray at the foot of the pitiful-looking statue.

When I was forced to leave Rwanda in 1998 because of death threats I'd received (yet another upsetting result of the genocide), I was determined to say good-bye to Our Lady of Kibeho. The problem was that I had a job and was nearly seven months pregnant with my first child, Nikki. And then, a week before I left, I saw a bus marked KIBEHO parked in front of my office at the United Nations. So I did what I'd done when I was in university: I got on the bus and played hooky to visit Mary.

The vehicle was an ancient minibus with no rear suspension, and it made many out-of-the-way stops along the rough roads. I had a slight medical condition that was going to make labor difficult, so my obstetrician had warned me not to do anything more strenuous than stand up from a chair. As I bounced up and down in that bus for three hours, I thought I'd go into early labor. When it got stuck in a mud hole and I had to get out and push with the others, I was sure that the baby would come prematurely.

Of course I would never do anything that would endanger the precious life inside of me; I was on a mission to see my Mother Mary and knew with absolute certainty that, as a mother herself, she wouldn't let any harm come to my baby. So when I finally arrived in Kibeho, I closed my eyes in front of the Blessed Virgin's statue and asked her to bless and care for my unborn child. Sure enough, my beautiful little girl would go on to be born in America . . . arriving two weeks later than expected, but healthy and well.

Before I left Kibeho that day, I looked around the muddied hills where the bones of the dead still protruded. I was reminded of my father's many wonderful stories of the love he'd felt here, of the miracles in the sky, of the messages that for years seemed to put a song of thanks in the hearts of everyone in the country. And then I thought about the warnings that had gone unheeded, along with the shattered lives and ruined country we'd inherited for not listening when heaven spoke to us.

I looked up at Mary, and this time I prayed out loud. "Good-bye, Mother. I hope that if I ever come back here, you won't be so sad and lonely," I told her. "I'll pray that they build you the home you asked for so that the world can come and see you. I'll pray that your messengers and your messages won't be forgotten. And, dear Mother, please pray for me."

EPILOGUE

---------- ❦ ----------

The New Jerusalem

Like all of Rwanda, Kibeho was nearly completely decimated by genocide.

But because the Blessed Mother's love is eternal and irrepressible, her spirit broke through the scorched and hardened earth and pushed up toward heaven, like a beautiful flower that would blossom with a thousand miracles.

Today, Kibeho is once again alive with the same fervor and passion that drew hundreds of thousands of Rwandans during the height of the apparitions in the 1980s. Once again pilgrims are flocking to the site where messages and miracles flowed so freely to any heart willing to receive them. Now the believers come not only from Rwanda, but from across Africa as well—people are even coming from as far away as Europe and America. Word has definitely spread that something wonderful, something *miraculous,* is happening in Kibeho.

At long last the fruit from those apparitions is being tasted by those hungry for God. This harvest has been in the making for more than a generation, becoming a reality in 2001. After 20 long years of investigation, the Church finally proclaimed that the evidence it had collected on the apparitions was too overwhelming to ignore: Mary appeared at Kibeho, the miracle is real, her messages are true, and the world must hear her words and feel the love the Queen of Heaven brought to share.

Bishop Augustin Misago made the announcement, declaring the apparitions of the original three visionaries from Kibeho High School—Alphonsine, Anathalie, and Marie-Claire—to be authentic. The messages received by the other visionaries (and the apparitions of Jesus) could be reexamined in further detail and perhaps approved in the future, but the construction of the chapel that Our Lady told Anathalie she wanted built was to begin immediately.

Three days after the bishop's announcement, the Vatican also added Kibeho to the very short, very select list of authorized Marian apparition sites, which include Fátima and Lourdes. Kibeho is in an even more exclusive club because it's the first and only approved Marian site on the African continent.

After so many years of painful and bitter divisiveness, Rwandans rallied together for Mary. Their voices were once again raised in unison, sharing the songs that the Holy Mother personally brought from heaven for them to sing.

Six months after the bishop's announcement, at least 50,000 of my compatriots stood in the driving rain during a special and joyous Mass in Kibeho. The were celebrating the day when the Mother of the Word appeared to Alphonsine at the high school, which had happened exactly 25 years earlier.

"Our Lady of Kibeho is a beacon of hope, a light for all of Africa and the world!" Bishop Misago emotionally declared to the thousands gathered at the celebration.

Since then, the little village has exploded in a whirl of spiritual activity, along with the heavy construction projects needed to accommodate the growing number of pilgrims—a number that's increasing exponentially as reports of miraculous cures and visions of Mary and Jesus appearing in the sky are carried to distant shores by those who have witnessed or experienced them personally.

A shrine dedicated to "Our Lady of Sorrows" is now located on the spot where the visionaries received their apparitions. And if you stand where the podium once was, you'll find yourself looking up at a statue of Mary. She is standing upon a pedestal, hovering ten feet in the air, appearing to all who gaze upon her as she did to the visionaries during their apparitions.

Across from the school sits the Church of the Seven Sorrows, named in honor of the special rosary the Blessed Mother taught Marie-Claire so that she, in turn, could teach it to the world. Inside is another statue of the Holy Virgin, dressed in white and blue, as she appeared to Anathalie.

But Mary is not alone; she's watched over by her son. Just a mile from the shrine, a magnificent bronze statue of "the Divine Mercy of Jesus" faces Our Lady of Sorrows. Weighing two tons and standing 18 feet tall, it's the largest statue of its kind in the world. Its message is simple: God loves us and His mercy is greater than our sins, so we must call upon Him with trust, receive His mercy, and let it flow through us to others.

The statue graces the entrance to CANA, a center run by Father Leszek Czelusniak, a wonderful friend of mine and a priest in the order of Marian Fathers. He came to Kibeho for a casual visit some years ago, and like so many who walk its hallowed ground, he felt the

Blessed Mother tug at his heart and whisper in his ear that Kibeho is where he belonged and was needed.

Putting his trust in God, Father Leszek has worked miracles raising money (often a nickel at a time) to build schools for local children and orphans, as well as chapels and guest rooms for distant travelers making the pilgrimage to Kibeho. Hundreds of local residents have joined Leszek—working together, brick by brick, they're moving toward fulfilling Our Lady's desire that one day Kibeho would be called the New Jerusalem.

Heaven sent its queen to Kibeho to bring us messages of truth and teach us the power of love and faith. That power still radiates through the sky and in the ground, as well as in the hearts of all those who make the pilgrimage to this holy place. I hope my words will convince some of you to make that special pilgrimage. Perhaps when you do, the money will have been found to build the basilica Our Lady requested, and it will greet you atop the hill like the castle of God I envisioned as a youngster.

Mary promised that Kibeho would be visited by millions of people from every corner of the world, and that those who sought her comfort and love would be heartened by the great strength of her faith.

She is there now, waiting, calling to the world to come to her to receive blessings beyond imagination. Who can refuse her when she calls? She may be Our Lady of Kibeho, but she is also the Blessed Mother of the entire world.

How to Pray
the Rosary of the Seven Sorrows

1. On the large medal at the bottom of the rosary:
   a. Make the sign of the cross.
   b. Say the Introductory Prayer.
   c. Say the Act of Contrition.

2. For each of the next three beads, say a Hail Mary.

3. On the first small medal:
   a. Say the prayer, "Most merciful mother, remind us always about the sorrows of your son, Jesus."
   b. Meditate upon the First Sorrowful Mystery.
   c. Say the Lord's Prayer.

4. For each of the next seven beads, say a Hail Mary.

5. On the second small medal:
   a. Say the prayer, "Most merciful mother . . . "
   b. Meditate upon the Second Sorrowful Mystery.
   c. Say the Lord's Prayer.

6. For each of the next seven beads, say a Hail Mary.

7. On the third small medal:
   a. Say the prayer, "Most merciful mother . . . "
   b. Meditate upon the Third Sorrowful Mystery.
   c. Say the Lord's Prayer.

8. For each of the next seven beads, say a Hail Mary.

9. On the fourth small medal:
   a. Say the prayer, "Most merciful mother . . . "
   b. Meditate upon the Fourth Sorrowful Mystery.
   c. Say the Lord's Prayer.

10. For each of the next seven beads, say a Hail Mary.

11. On the fifth small medal:
    a. Say the prayer, "Most merciful mother . . . "
    b. Meditate upon the Fifth Sorrowful Mystery.
    c. Say the Lord's Prayer.

12. For each of the next seven beads, say a Hail Mary.

13. On the sixth small medal:
    a. Say the prayer, "Most merciful mother . . . "
    b. Meditate upon the Sixth Sorrowful Mystery.
    c. Say the Lord's Prayer.

14. For each of the next seven beads, say a Hail Mary.

15. On the seventh small medal:
    a. Say the prayer, "Most merciful mother . . . "
    b. Meditate upon the Seventh Sorrowful Mystery.
    c. Say the Lord's Prayer.

16. For each of the next seven beads, say a Hail Mary.

17. Upon reaching the large medal at the bottom of the rosary:
    a. Say the prayer, "Most merciful mother . . . "
    b. Say the Concluding Prayer.
    c. Say three times: "Mary, who was conceived without sin and who suffered for us, pray for us."

Make a sign of the cross; your prayers will be answered!

THE ROSARY OF
THE SEVEN SORROWS

◦━◦━◦━◦━◦ ❀ ◦━◦━◦━◦━◦

This rosary recalls the seven major sorrows that the Virgin Mary suffered through—albeit with love and compassion—during the life, trials, and agonizing death of her son, Jesus Christ. It's very special to the immaculate heart of the Blessed Mother, and she wants all of us to say it as often as possible.

The Rosary of the Seven Sorrows dates back to the Middle Ages, but it gained new popularity following the Marian apparitions in Kibeho, which have been approved by the Catholic Church. During Mary's apparitions to Marie-Claire Mukangango, she assigned the young visionary a mission to reintroduce this special rosary to the world. Before her untimely death, Marie-Claire did just that, traveling widely to teach it to thousands of people, who then taught it to thousands of others.

During her visitations to Kibeho, the Holy Virgin revealed that this rosary possesses immense spiritual power for those who say it sincerely. She promised that when prayed with an open and repentant heart, the rosary would win us the Lord's forgiveness for our sins and free our souls from guilt and remorse. She also promised that over time, the rosary would develop within us a deep understanding of *why* we sin, and that knowledge would give us the wisdom and strength to change or remove any internal flaws, weaknesses of character, or personality faults causing unhappiness and keeping us from enjoying the joyous life God intended for us to live.

The Rosary of the Seven Sorrows contains all the power you need to change your life for the better, obtain peace and happiness, realize your true potential, fulfill all your dreams, and grow closer to God's light. During one of her many apparitions to Marie-Claire, the Holy Virgin suggested that it be prayed as often as possible, but especially on Tuesdays and Fridays: Tuesday being the day Mary first appeared to Marie-Claire, and Friday being the day Christ was crucified. The Blessed Mother also stressed that the Rosary of the Seven Sorrows is intended to complement—*and in no way replace*—the traditional rosary. Pray both rosaries regularly and you'll be doubly blessed!

The following is a description of this amazing rosary as the Virgin Mother herself taught it to Marie-Claire in Kibeho. It may be prayed aloud or contemplated silently, alone or with others; the key is for the prayers, reflections, and meditations to always come from the depths of your heart.

I speak from experience when I promise that you'll never regret learning this wonderful rosary and that you'll soon lose track of the countless blessings that praying it will bring into your life. It's my hope that more people than ever before will learn just how amazing this rosary is.

Please note that you don't necessarily need any special beads to say these prayers; just follow the diagram and instructions on page 186. (It is, however, important that when you reach each sorrowful mystery, you take a moment to meditate on the magnitude of Mary's suffering . . . and the strength of her love.)

— **Introductory Prayer:** *My God, I offer You this rosary for Your glory, so I may honor Your Holy Mother, the Blessed Virgin, so I can share and meditate upon her suffering. I humbly beg You to give me true repentance for all my sins. Give me wisdom and humility so that I may receive all the indulgences contained in this prayer.*

— **Act of Contrition:** *O my God, I am heartily sorry for having offended You, and I detest all my sins because I dread the loss of heaven and the pains of hell; but most of all because they offend You, my God, You Who are all good and deserving of all my love. I firmly resolve, with the help of Your grace, to confess my sins, to do penance, and to amend my life. Amen.*

— **Before Each Mystery, Pray:** *Most merciful mother, remind us always about the sorrows of your son, Jesus.*

1. The First Sorrowful Mystery:
The Prophecy of Simeon (Luke 2:22–35)

The Blessed Virgin Mary took Jesus to the temple, as tradition demanded that all newborns be blessed in the temple before God. There, the old priest Simeon held the baby Jesus in his hands, and the Holy Spirit filled his heart. Simeon recognized Jesus as the promised Savior and held the child high toward heaven, thanking God for granting his wish that he would live long enough to behold the Messiah.

"Now Your servant may depart this life in peace, my Lord," he said. Then he looked upon Mary and proclaimed, "And you, woman, a sword of sorrow will pierce your heart because of the suffering that shall befall your child."

The Blessed Virgin knew that she had given birth to the Savior of humankind, so she immediately understood and accepted Simeon's prophecy. Although her heart was deeply touched by this favor of bearing the baby Jesus, her heart remained heavy and troubled, for she knew what had been written about the ordeals and subsequent death of the Savior. Whenever she saw her son, she was constantly reminded of the suffering he would be subjected to, and his suffering became her own.

Prayer: *Beloved Mother Mary, whose heart suffered beyond bearing because of us, teach us to suffer with you and with love, and to accept all the suffering God deems it necessary to send our way. Let us suffer, and may our suffering be known to God only, like yours and that of Jesus. Do not let us show our suffering to the world, so it will matter more and be used to atone for the sins of the world. You, Mother, who suffered with the Savior of the world, we offer you our suffering, and the suffering of the world, because we are your children. Join those sorrows to your own and to those of the Lord Jesus Christ, then offer them to God the Father so that He will know the one who created it. You are a mother greater than all.*

2. The Second Sorrowful Mystery: The Flight into Egypt (Matthew 2:13–15)

Mary's heart broke and her mind was greatly troubled when Joseph revealed to her the words of the angel:

they were to wake up quickly and flee to Egypt because Herod wanted to kill Jesus. The Blessed Virgin hardly had time to decide what to take or leave behind; she took her child and left everything else, rushing outside before Joseph so that they could hurry as God wished. Then she said, "Even though God has power over everything, He wants us to flee with Jesus, His son. God will show us the way, and we shall arrive without being caught by the enemy."

Because the Blessed Virgin was the mother of Jesus, she loved him more than anyone else. Her heart was deeply troubled at the sight of her infant son's discomfort, and she suffered greatly because he was cold and shivering. While she and her husband were tired, sleepy, and hungry during this long travel, Mary's only thought was about the safety and comfort of her child. She feared coming face-to-face with the soldiers who had been ordered to kill Jesus because she was aware that the enemy was still in Bethlehem. Her heart remained constantly anguished during this flight. She also knew that where they were going, there would be no friendly faces to greet them.

Prayer: *Beloved Mother, who has suffered so much, give to us your courageous heart. Give us strength so that we can be brave like you and accept with love the suffering God sends our way. Help us to also accept all the suffering we inflict upon ourselves and the suffering inflicted upon us by others. Heavenly Mother, you alone purify our suffering so that we may give glory to God and save our souls.*

3. The Third Sorrowful Mystery:
The Loss of Jesus in the Temple (Luke 2:41–52)

Jesus was the only begotten son of God, but he was also Mary's child. The Blessed Virgin loved Jesus more than herself because he was her God. Compared to other children, he was most unique because he was already living as God. When Mary lost Jesus on their way back from Jerusalem, the world became so big and lonely that she believed she couldn't go on living without him, so great was her sorrow. (She felt the same pain her son felt when he was later abandoned by his apostles during the Passion.)

As the Holy Mother looked anxiously for her beloved boy, deep pain welled in her heart. She blamed herself, asking why she didn't take greater care of him. But it was not her fault; Jesus no longer needed her protection as before. What really hurt Mary was that her son had decided to stay behind without her consent. Jesus had pleased her in everything so far: he never annoyed her in any way, nor would he ever displease his parents. She knew that he always did what was necessary, however, so she never suspected him of being disobedient.

Prayer: *Beloved Mother, teach us to accept all our sufferings because of our sins and to atone for the sins of the whole world.*

4. The Fourth Sorrowful Mystery:
Mary Meets Jesus on the Way to Calvary
(Luke 23:27–31)

Mary witnessed Jesus carrying the heavy cross alone—the cross on which he was to be crucified. This didn't surprise the Blessed Virgin because she already knew about the approaching death of Our Lord. Noting how her son was already weakened by the numerous hard blows given by the soldiers' clubs, she was filled with anguish at his pain.

The soldiers kept hurrying and pushing him, though he had no strength left. He fell, exhausted, unable to raise himself. At that moment, Mary's eyes, so full of tender love and compassion, met her son's eyes, which were pained and covered in blood. Their hearts seemed to be sharing the load; every pain he felt, she felt as well. They knew that nothing could be done except to believe and trust in God and dedicate their suffering to Him. All they could do was put everything in God's hands.

Prayer: *Beloved Mother, so stricken with grief, help us to bear our own suffering with courage and love so that we may relieve your sorrowful heart and that of Jesus. In doing so, may we give glory to God Who gave you and Jesus to humanity. As you suffered, teach us to suffer silently and patiently. Grant unto us the grace of loving God in everything. O Mother of Sorrows, most afflicted of all mothers, have mercy on the sinners of the whole world.*

5. The Fifth Sorrowful Mystery:
Mary Stands at the Foot of the Cross
(John 19:25–27)

The Blessed Virgin Mary continued to climb the mount to Calvary, following behind Jesus painfully and sorrowfully, yet suffering silently. She could see him staggering and falling with the cross some more, and she witnessed her son being beaten by soldiers who pulled his hair to force him to stand up.

Despite his innocence, when Jesus reached the top of Calvary, he was ordered to confess in front of the crowd so they could laugh at him. Mary deeply felt her son's pain and humiliation, particularly when his tormentors forced him to strip off what was left of his clothing. The Blessed Virgin felt sick at heart seeing these tyrants crucifying her son naked, shaming him terribly merely to amuse the jeering crowd. (Jesus and Mary felt more disgrace than normal people did because they were holy and without sin.)

The Blessed Virgin Mary felt pain beyond bearing when Jesus was stretched out on the cross. His murderers sang merrily as they approached him with hammers and nails. They sat on him heavily so that he could not move when they spiked him to the wood. As they hammered the nails through his hands and feet, Mary felt the blows in her heart; the nails pierced her flesh as they tore into her son's body. She felt her life fading away.

As the soldiers lifted the cross to drop it into the hole they'd dug, they deliberately jerked it, causing the force of Jesus's bodily weight to tear through the flesh on his hands and expose his bone. The pain shot through his body like liquid fire. He endured three excruciating hours skewered on the cross, yet the physical pain was nothing compared to the agonizing heartache he was forced to bear seeing his mother suffering below him. Mercifully, he finally died.

❀

Prayer: *Beloved Mother, Queen of the Martyrs, give us the courage you had in all your sufferings so that we may unite our sufferings with yours and give glory to God. Help us follow all His commandments and those of the Church so that Our Lord's sacrifice will not be in vain, and all sinners in the world will be saved.*

6. The Sixth Sorrowful Mystery:
Mary Receives the Dead Body of Jesus in Her Arms
(John 19:38–40)

The friends of Jesus, Joseph and Nicodemus, took down his body from the cross and placed it in the outstretched arms of the Blessed Virgin. Then Mary washed it with deep respect and love because she was his mother. She knew better than anyone else that he was God incarnate who'd taken a human body to become the Savior of all people.

Mary could see the terrifying wounds from the flogging Jesus had received while at Pilate's. His flesh had been shredded and large strips had been torn from his back. His entire body had been so lacerated that gaping wounds crisscrossed him from head to toe. Mary found that the wounds from the nails were less severe than those caused by the flogging and by carrying the cross. She was horrified at the thought that her son had managed to carry the heavy, splintered cross all the way to Calvary. She saw the circle of blood the crown of thorns had made on his forehead and, to her horror, realized that many of the barbed thorns had dug so deeply into his skull they had penetrated his brain.

Looking at her broken boy, the Holy Mother knew that his agonizing death was far worse than the torture reserved for the wickedest of criminals. As she cleaned his damaged body, she envisioned him during each stage of his short life, remembering her first look at his beautiful newborn face as the two of them lay in the manger, and every day in between, until this heartrending moment as she gently bathed his lifeless body. Her anguish was relentless as she prepared her son and Lord for burial, but she remained brave and strong, becoming the true Queen of Martyrs. As she washed her son, she prayed that everybody would know the riches of paradise and enter the gates of heaven. She prayed for every soul in the world to embrace God's love so her son's torturous death would benefit all humankind and would not have been in vain. Mary prayed for the world; she prayed for all of us.

❦

Prayer: *We thank you, Beloved Mother, for your courage as you stood beneath your dying child to comfort him on the cross. As our Savior drew his last breath, you became a wonderful mother to all of us; you became the Blessed Mother of the world. We know that you love us more than our own earthly parents do. We implore you to be our advocate before the throne of mercy and grace so that we can truly become your children. We thank you for Jesus, our Savior and Redeemer, and we thank Jesus for giving you to us. Please pray for us, Mother.*

7. The Seventh Sorrowful Mystery:
Jesus Is Placed in the Tomb (John 19:41–42)

The life of the Blessed Virgin Mary was so closely linked to that of Jesus she thought there was no reason for her to go on living any longer. Her only comfort was that his death had ended his unspeakable suffering. Our sorrowful mother, with the help of John and the holy women, devoutly placed Jesus's body in the sepulchre, and she left him there as any other dead person. She went home with great pain and tremendous sorrow; for the first time she was without him, and her loneliness was a new and bitter source of pain. Her heart had been dying since her son's heart had stopped beating, but she was certain that our Savior would soon be resurrected.

Prayer: *Most Beloved Mother, whose beauty surpassed that of all mothers, mother of mercy, mother of Jesus, and mother to us all, we are your children and we place all our trust in you. Teach us to see God in all things and all situations, even in our sufferings. Help us to understand the importance of suffering, and also to know the purpose of our suffering as God had intended it.*

You yourself were conceived and born without sin, were preserved from sin, yet you suffered more than anybody else has. You accepted suffering and pain with love and with unsurpassed courage. You stood by your son from the time he was arrested until he died. You suffered along with him, felt every pain and torment he did. You accomplished the will of God the Father; and according to His will, you have become our savior with Jesus. We beg you, dear Mother, to teach us to do as Jesus did. Teach us to accept our cross courageously. We trust you, most merciful mother, so teach us to sacrifice for all the sinners in the world. Help us to follow in your son's footsteps, and even to be willing to lay down our lives for others.

— **Concluding Prayer:** *Queen of Martyrs, your heart suffered so much. I beg you, by the merits of the tears you shed in these terrible and sorrowful times, to obtain for me and all the sinners of the world the grace of complete sincerity and repentance. Amen.*

Three times, say: *Mary, who was conceived without sin and who suffered for us, pray for us.*

Congratulations on finishing the Rosary of the Seven Sorrows of the Virgin Mary! Now make the sign of the cross to wipe away the tears Mary shed during the Passion of Jesus, and rest assured that your prayers will be answered!

ACKNOWLEDGMENTS

To dear God Almighty, thank You for sending the Virgin Mary and Your son to visit our country, which so desperately needed You then and still does now. Thank You for revealing Your tender love to us through the purest of souls, the Blessed Mother. I love You with all my heart, dear Father, but as I do every day, I beg You to increase my capacity to love You even more. You, upon whom the whole world depends, I entrust with my every breath.

To my dearest heavenly Mother, the Blessed Virgin Mary, Our Lady of Kibeho, please accept this tribute from your adoring daughter, this love letter from one of your many little flowers. This is my simple way of saying thank you for the love and kindness you've blessed me with throughout my life, of showing appreciation for the adoration you lavished on us all by visiting our modest country and trusting us to do as you asked by delivering your messages to the world.

This book is for you, dear Mother. Thank you for allowing me to serve as your humble messenger, and please forgive me if my words fail to express the depth of love and compassion you and Jesus possess for your children. Mother, you know my heart knows no limit for loving you, but it does suffer limitations when attempting to describe your own heavenly love while using the feeble languages we fumble with on Earth. I respectfully request you to intercede on my behalf to ensure that God's grace touches all who read these pages—help them discover the great truth and beauty of your loving messages.

Please, dear Mother, fill in any blanks I've left with your tender love so that other people will truly feel the warmth and safety of being in your presence. If just one person can sense the purity of your love by reading these words, they'll know that they need never feel lonely or sad again because you're always beside them, holding their hand and touching their heart . . . if that were to happen, dear lady, my reason for writing this book would have been fulfilled.

To Reid Tracy, thank you with all my heart for doing the impossible by helping me honor the Feast of Our Lady of Kibeho with this book, and for enabling me to keep my promise to our Heavenly Mother that I would share her message with as many souls as possible. May God reward you a thousand times, and a thousand times more, for listening to His voice and overcoming every outside obstacle placed in your path. Reid, you know more than many that with God, all things are possible.

Thank you to the wonderful Jill Kramer, for her tireless efforts to make this dream of mine come true. And a huge thank you to all the hardworking folks at Hay House who have labored so hard on this book—may the Virgin Mary wrap you in her loving arms and bless you with happiness for your efforts. Thanks especially to Charles McStravick for creating such an amazing design for the cover; your talent allows Our Lady of Kibeho to beckon all who pass her on the bookshelf and draw them in to her story.

To Wayne Dyer, thank you for your boundless energy and passion when it comes to serving humanity; your work and enthusiasm help so many people find peace, security, and happiness. You have a true gift for putting smiles on faces, and the world is a better place for having you in it. And I have to thank you again and again for being so kind and generous to me. You gave me a voice and brought my story to the world, and for that I am forever grateful. Nothing gives me greater pleasure than when I hear your name mentioned in conversation and can proudly say that you are my dear, dear friend.

To Maya, you are a rare and precious pearl; I treasure your magnificent heart and bless you for remaining my constant guardian angel.

To Steve Erwin, well, we did it again! I've been waiting to write this book with you, and now we've done it—what a miraculous achievement. The most exciting thing about this project for me was being able to introduce you to my most tender mother, Our Lady of Kibeho. I hope that writing this book with me has been as much a gift for you as it has been for me. Thank you for always making yourself available to me, first by sharing the sorrow of my heart in *Left to Tell*; then by accompanying me on my healing journey in *Led by Faith*; and now for being my traveling companion on the most exciting voyage yet, as I return to the source of my strength and secret happiness and visit the one who has inspired all I've done, Our Lady of Kibeho. We are truly sister and brother now, Steve, because we share the same wonderful mother! And, of course, I still look upon your beautiful wife, Natasha, as a sister.

To my dear friend Amy, thank you for being the sister I never had. Thank you for saying yes to Our Lady of Kibeho. I love you.

To my friend Tim, thank you for your constant support and love, as well as your companionship. For your passion in supporting Our Lady of Kibeho and all your selfless effort, you will be rewarded. I love you and your wonderful family for being such supportive parents.

Thank you to Bill and Carol for all your love as well, and for your love for Kibeho. I'm grateful to have you in my life.

To Ed Wards, thank you for all your help and kindness, and for relating with such heartfelt enthusiasm to my story. I will thank you forever.

To Lionel Fundira, thank you for taking the time to go over my words and offer such good advice.

To my dear friend Phuong Tran, where would I be without you? Thank you for keeping me organized, on track, and (as often as possible) on time!

To my dear brother Aimable, I hope that you'll read this book with a smile and without the painful memories of our family story. Thank you for being proud of me and for not wavering from being the loving and caring big brother you've been since I was born. You mean the world to me, and I thank God for keeping you alive through all that happened to our family. Bless you, brother; and bless your beautiful wife, Sauda, who is no longer my sister-in-law but has become my sister-in-heart.

To my dear little angels, Nikki and B.J., my babies, I love you always—you are my sunshine and the loves of my life. You make my heart smile every moment of every day, and your love keeps me alive.

To my little nephew, Ryan, you are my lucky charm and darling boy. And to the latest addition to the family, sweet little Loanna, you are the youngest and brightest star in our expanding universe and will light the way to our family's future. Your aunt loves you very much, and as soon as you learn to talk, I will tell you lots of embarrassing stories about your daddy! We are going to be great friends, my sweetheart!

To my cousin Pauline, I love you and can't get over the fact that you're a grown woman about to get married. How did that happen? When did you become so smart, beautiful, gentle, and kind? I am so very proud of you! To Stephane, what a joy to see you two together. Thank you for extending our family; I couldn't ask for a better brother-in-law or better husband for my little cousin. I am blessed to have both of you, and may God bless your life together.

To Oscar, thank you so much for presenting Kibeho with the magnificent gift of the truly remarkable statue of the Divine Mercy of Jesus. You'll never know how deeply my country has been affected by your generosity: hundreds of healings have happened beneath that glorious image of Christ already, and in the years to come there will be tens of thousands of miracles in that remarkable spot. It is a gift from God, and I thank you for your kindness and for being a great and true friend.

To my dear, dear Father Leszek, I don't have words to thank you for what you've done for Kibeho and continue to do. You truly are doing the Lord's work in that blessed spot, and I pray that our beloved Blessed Mother who summoned you to Kibeho continues to bless and guide you and your work. Your continuous effort to master Rwanda's native language proves to me that you're a soul who's been sent to us to genuinely help. My gratitude goes out to all the missionaries who are helping build up Kibeho, especially Father Paul and the Pallottine fathers. Sister Raphael, you are a star; thank you for your work supporting the blind in Rwanda.

To Augustin Misago, the Bishop of Gikongoro, I thank you with all my heart for all your efforts in speeding up the studies on the Kibeho apparitions and visionaries, along with all you've done to ensure that it became (and will forever remain) a holy site of Marian apparition. Thank you for sharing your time and invaluable insights that helped so much in shaping this book. No doubt God has wisely chosen you to be the shepherd of His flock in this special place.

And please, dearest excellency, accept my humble request in the name of the thousands of pilgrims who came to Kibeho all those years ago and heard the messages of visionaries other than the three so far approved: so many of us believe that the Virgin Mary delivered genuine messages to at least five other visionaries, which must be heard by the world. As you know, tens of thousands also believe that Jesus appeared in Kibeho, too, with messages that are critical for the times in which we live. You haven't denied the validity of any visionary, and I pray that you keep an open heart and mind; and in the near future, you decide to resume the official investigations of those who carried messages of vital importance for the world. We, the friends of Kibeho, beg you to look again at the other visionaries and ensure that the messages they received from Our Mother and Our Lord are made public and heard by those for whom they were intended. I know that Our Lady of Kibeho will assist in this work—she always does.

A very special thanks to the exceptional soul who's too humble to reveal your name in public, the anonymous donor of remarkable generosity who parted so freely with the money to build a lovely and sacred chapel in Kibeho. God bless you for your lasting gift and your true humility.

To all the visionaries in Kibeho, thank you for offering yourselves as instruments of Our Lady and bravely enduring so much torment and humiliation in the beginning—torment that continues to haunt many of you to this day. Thank you for all of your sufferings for humanity; your reward in heaven will surely be great.

And may God, Jesus, the Blessed Mother, and all the angels and saints in heaven watch over the visionaries whose lives were taken during the genocide, as well as those who were taken to their reward through illness. The world thanks you for speaking the truth; Rwanda thanks you for your piety and strength; and I thank you for filling the heart of a child with the love of Our Lady, and for setting me on the road to God.

To the countless thousands of pilgrims who have trekked to Kibeho over the years, you know more than anyone that walking this hallowed ground is spiritu ally transformative. Our Lady of Kibeho calls out to her children across the world to visit her at her holy shrine, and those who answer her call are blessed for life. No one who journeys to Kibeho ever truly leaves, for once you've seen Kibeho, it will touch your heart and stay with you forever.

Finally, to all of you who read this book, I pray that in these pages you've found inspiration, a renewal of faith, and a sense of the true joy waiting for you just a prayer away. To those of you who have discovered (or been reunited with) Our Blessed Mother through this work, I ask you to keep me in your prayers, for I will most certainly keep you in mine. May God bless you and those you hold dear through all the days of your life.

I love you all.

— **Immaculée**

My dear Immaculée, thank you for always brightening my life, and bless you for introducing me to Mary. She has touched me deeply; I think this is the beginning of a beautiful friendship.

Thanks to Jill Kramer at Hay House for being a consummate pro and a true inspiration, and for cultivating the patience of Job. It is always a pleasure working with you. Many thanks as well to Reid Tracy for his great work. And a huge thanks to Shannon Littrell, a fine editor and a real corker. Also thanks to Christy Salinas, Jami Goddess, and every other member of the extraordinary team at Hay House.

As always, much gratitude to Faith Farthing of FinalEyes Communications in Edmonton—your eyes are as sharp as ever and insights spot-on. I'm always confident you'd never leave a comma out of place or a participle dangling out in space. You've tidied and improved my work for 16 years, and I look forward to 16 more.

To my beautiful and talented wife of ten wonderful years, Natasha Stoynoff, my heart still belongs to you (and shall forever)—do with it what you will.

— Steve Erwin

ABOUT THE AUTHORS

Immaculée Ilibagiza was born in Rwanda and studied electronic and mechanical engineering at the National University. She lost most of her family during the 1994 genocide. Four years later, she emigrated to the United States and soon began working at the United Nations in New York City. She is now a full-time public speaker and writer. In 2007 she established the Left to Tell Charitable Fund, which helps support Rwandan orphans.

Immaculée holds honorary doctoral degrees from the University of Notre Dame and St. John's University, and was awarded the Mahatma Gandhi International Award for Reconciliation and Peace in 2007. She is the author, with Steve Erwin, of *Left to Tell* and *Led by Faith*.

To help fulfill Our Lady's vision for Kibeho as a New Jerusalem—where the poor, displaced, and spiritually hungry of the world can gather to worship, find comfort, and be healed at a beautiful shrine and welcoming basilica—please visit the foundation Immaculée has created for that purpose at: **www.ourladyofkibeho.com**.

To find out what she's doing to help spread the important messages of love and hope that Our Lady delivered in Kibeho for the entire world to hear, please visit her own Website: **www.immaculee.com**.

Steve Erwin is a Toronto-born writer and award-winning journalist working in the print and broadcast media. Most recently, he was the New York foreign correspondent for the Canadian Broadcasting Corporation. He co-authored the *New York Times* best-selling memoirs *Left to Tell* and *Led by Faith*. He lives in Manhattan with his wife, journalist and author Natasha Stoynoff.

NOTES

NOTES

NOTES

NOTES

NOTES

NOTES

We hope you enjoyed this Hay House book.
If you'd like to receive our online catalog featuring additional
information on Hay House books and products, or if you'd like to find
out more about the Hay Foundation, please contact:

Hay House, Inc.
P.O. Box 5100
Carlsbad, CA 92018-5100

(760) 431-7695 or **(800) 654-5126**
(760) 431-6948 (fax) or **(800) 650-5115 (fax)**
www.hayhouse.com® • **www.hayfoundation.org**

Published and distributed in Australia by: Hay House Australia Pty.
Ltd., 18/36 Ralph St., Alexandria NSW 2015 • *Phone:* 612-9669-4299
Fax: 612-9669-4144 • www.hayhouse.com.au

Published and distributed in the United Kingdom by:
Hay House UK, Ltd., Astley House, 33 Notting Hill Gate, London W11 3JQ
Phone: 44-20-3675-2450 • *Fax:* 44-20-3675-2451 • www.hayhouse.co.uk

Published and distributed in the Republic of South Africa by:
Hay House SA (Pty), Ltd., P.O. Box 990, Witkoppen 2068
Phone/Fax: 27-11-467-8904 • www.hayhouse.co.za

Published in India by: Hay House Publishers India, Muskaan
Complex, Plot No. 3, B-2, Vasant Kunj, New Delhi 110 070 • *Phone:*
91-11-4176-1620 • *Fax:* 91-11-4176-1630 • www.hayhouse.co.in

Distributed in Canada by: Raincoast Books, 2440 Viking Way,
Richmond, B.C. V6V 1N2 • *Phone:* 1-800-663-5714
Fax: 1-800-565-3770 • www.raincoast.com

Take Your Soul on a Vacation

Visit **www.HealYourLife.com®** to regroup, recharge, and reconnect
with your own magnificence. Featuring blogs, mind-body-spirit news,
and life-changing wisdom from Louise Hay and friends.

Visit **www.HealYourLife.com** today!

Free e-newsletters from Hay House, the Ultimate Resource for Inspiration

Be the first to know about Hay House's dollar deals, free downloads, special offers, affirmation cards, giveaways, contests, and more!

 Get exclusive excerpts from our latest releases and videos from *Hay House Present Moments*.

 Enjoy uplifting personal stories, how-to articles, and healing advice, along with videos and empowering quotes, within *Heal Your Life*.

 Have an inspirational story to tell and a passion for writing? Sharpen your writing skills with insider tips from *Your Writing Life*.

Sign Up Now!

Get inspired, educate yourself, get a complimentary gift, and share the wisdom!

http://www.hayhouse.com/newsletters.php

Visit www.hayhouse.com to sign up today!

 HAY HOUSE

HAYHOUSE RADIO
radio for your soul

HealYourLife.com ♥

Heal Your Life One Thought at a Time . . . on Louise's All-New Website!

"*Life is bringing me everything I need and more.*"

— Louise Hay

Come to HEALYOURLIFE.COM today and meet the world's best-selling self-help authors; the most popular leading intuitive, health, and success experts; up-and-coming inspirational writers; and new like-minded friends who will share their insights, experiences, personal stories, and wisdom so you can heal your life and the world around you . . . one thought at a time.

Here are just some of the things you'll get at HealYourLife.com:

- DAILY AFFIRMATIONS
- CAPTIVATING VIDEO CLIPS
- EXCLUSIVE BOOK REVIEWS
- AUTHOR BLOGS
- LIVE TWITTER AND FACEBOOK FEEDS
- BEHIND-THE-SCENES SCOOPS
- LIVE STREAMING RADIO
- "MY LIFE" COMMUNITY OF FRIENDS

PLUS:
FREE Monthly Contests and Polls
FREE BONUS gifts, discounts,
and newsletters

Make It Your Home Page Today!

www.HealYourLife.com®

HEAL YOUR LIFE®